A Guide to Neural
Computing Applications

A Guide to Neural Computing Applications

Lionel Tarassenko

Professor of Electrical and Electronic Engineering
University of Oxford
UK

A member of the Hodder Headline Group

LONDON • SYDNEY • AUCKLAND
Copublished in North, Central and South America by
John Wiley & Sons Inc., New York • Toronto

First published in Great Britain in 1998 by
Arnold, a member of the Hodder Headline Group,
338 Euston Road, London NW1 3BH
http://www.arnoldpublishers.com

Copublished in North, Central and South America by
John Wiley & Sons Inc.,
605 Third Street,
New York, NY 10158-0012

British Library Cataloguing in Publication Data
A catalogue record for this book is available from the British Library

Library of Congress Cataloging-in-Publication Data
A catalog record for this book is available from the Library of Congress

ISBN 0 340 70589 2
ISBN 0 471 25550 5 (Wiley)

Publisher: Eliane Wigzell
Production Editor: James Rabson
Production Controller: Priya Gohil
Cover designer: Terry Griffiths

Typeset in 10/12 pt Times by Focal Image, Torquay
Printed and bound in Great Britain by J W Arrowsmith, Bristol

CONTENTS

Foreword

Neural networks are fascinating. A few simple algorithms will learn relationships between cause and effect or organise large volumes of data into orderly and informative patterns. The prospects for commercial exploitation have been shown to be real over the past couple of years. It is easy to be carried away and begin to overestimate their capabilities. The usual consequence of this is, hopefully, no more serious than an embarrassing failure with concomitant mutterings about black boxes and excessive hype. Neural networks cannot solve every problem. Traditional methods may be better. Nevertheless, neural networks, when they are used wisely, usually perform at least as well as the most appropriate traditional method and in some cases significantly better.

In one sense neural networks are no more than just another statistical technique, just another systems identification tool, or another clustering algorithm or mapping function. In another sense they are revolutionary. They put the tool in the hands of the applications expert rather than the data analyst. In the terms of late 1980s business jargon, they 'enable the end user'. It is almost invariably much quicker for the engineer or scientist to learn how to use neural networks than it is for the data analyst to learn quantum electrodynamics. Of course the data analyst who does know quantum electrodynamics can, by adding neural networks to her armoury of techniques, quickly produce compact empirical models of high dimensional non-linear systems.

The Neural Computing Applications Forum commissioned this book for its members, who are a group of people interested in the effective application of neural networks. The book was inspired by a set of guidelines produced for the United Kingdom Government's Department of Trade and Industry as part of their Neural Computing Learning Solutions Initiative. Assignment of the copyright of the text of the original book is gratefully acknowledged. In taking account of the lessons learned over the very active years since the DTI guidelines were published, Professor Tarassenko has largely rewritten the original text and has provided new sample applications which are described in detail.

This book provides a set of guidelines which will help everyone make best use of neural networks. It will help people to avoid some of the obvious and not so obvious pitfalls which can lead to the unnecessary failure of projects. These guidelines will benefit the newcomer to neural computing who will be able to construct robust and meaningful non-linear models and classifiers. They will also benefit the more experienced practitioner who through over-familiarity with the subject might otherwise be inclined to jump to unwarranted conclusions on the basis of past experience with different applications. It should be an invaluable resource not only for those in industry who are interested in neural computing solutions but also for final-year undergraduates or graduate students who are working on neural computing projects or who wish to familiarise themselves with the subject.

This book is important for three reasons. It provides advice that will help us to make best use of the growing number of commercial and public domain neural network software products. It frees the medical, scientific, engineering or commercial specialist from dependence upon external consultants. Call upon the software house, contract research organisation or academic institution to advise on the best way to extract features or parameterise a problem if you wish. Do so as an informed customer, aware of the likely scale of the tasks involved and with the knowledge and skills that would enable you to do the task yourself if you desired. Finally, it is an opportunity to observe the thought processes of Professor Tarassenko, one of our foremost neural network practitioners. He leads an active research group at Oxford University. At the same time he uses his technical and communications skills to collaborate with industrial partners to implement neural network technology in commercial products and practical industrial applications.

Dr Peter Cowley
Chairman of The Neural Computing Applications Forum
Rolls-Royce Applied Science Laboratory
July 1997

1

INTRODUCTION

1.1 Neural computing—today's perspective

A decade ago, Lippmann wrote the following in a key review paper on Artificial
Neural Networks (Lippmann, 1987):

> 'Artificial neural net structure is based on our present understanding
> of biological nervous systems. Neural net models have greatest po-
> tential in areas such as speech and image recognition where many
> hypotheses are pursued in parallel, high computation rates are re-
> quired, and the current best systems are far from equalling human
> performance.'

The two main issues then in the resurgent field of neural network research were
the massive parallelism of neural network architectures (a characteristic shared
with networks of real neurons) and the newly-discovered means of training a
neural network to solve the Exclusive-OR problem. Ten years later, these issues
no longer dominate the field. For example, Bishop, in the preface to his book,
Neural Networks and Pattern Recognition (Bishop, 1995) makes the following
point:

> 'Historically, many concepts in neural computing have been inspired
> by studies of biological networks. The perspective of statistical pat-
> tern recognition, however, offers a much more direct and principled
> route to many of the same concepts.'

Does this statement represent a downbeat assessment with respect to Lippmann's
review a decade earlier? Far from it—the integration of (artificial) neural networks[1] within statistical pattern recognition has been the key development of
the past decade. The ability of neural networks such as Multi-Layer Perceptrons
(MLPs) or Radial Basis Function (RBF) networks to create non-linear decision
boundaries as a result of (relatively) simple training procedures has made it
possible to solve hard pattern recognition or signal analysis problems. Indeed,

---

[1]The qualifier *artificial* will be dropped from the rest of the book as it has fallen into disuse
over the last ten years.

one of the main aims of this book is to show how much can be achieved if MLPs and RBF networks are trained and used properly.

An important *caveat* must be introduced even at this early stage. The availability of a large number of software packages has paradoxically made the potential for the misuse of neural networks greater than ever. There is often a mistaken belief that all that is required to obtain meaningful results from a neural network package is a set of data and associated labels. This ignores two vital issues: whether or not there are sufficient data to train the network and how best to represent information about the problem domain at the input of the network. A secondary aim of this book, therefore, is to show, primarily through worked examples, the *correct* way to train a neural network and the pathologies which can arise as a result of *not* doing so.

1.2 The purpose of this book

This book concentrates on the very real *benefits* which neural networks can bring, if properly applied to the problem in question. The author of the book has been involved in a number of neural computing projects which have gone all the way from concept to product, for example the world's first microwave oven to be controlled by a neural network (the Sharp LogiCook) and a system to analyse sleep disorders now being sold world-wide by the Oxford Medical Division of Oxford Instruments. These *products* demonstrate that the principled use of neural computing can give novel, yet cost-effective, solutions in a commercial, rather than purely academic, context.

The book therefore concentrates on the *application* of neural networks, but such a focus should never be an excuse for operating outside a sound theoretical framework. The reader will therefore find the text liberally sprinkled with examples, most of which are based on real-world data sets (rather than synthetic toy problems). At the same time, he or she will also find that the chapter which immediately follows this introduction provides the mathematical framework for neural computing. Neural networks do *not* represent a generic black-box approach to the solution of apparently intractable problems, and it is important that every reader should understand this from the outset. It is not essential to follow in detail all of the mathematical derivations in Chapter 2 but it is vital to realise that the practical approach presented in the later chapters is based on the assumptions and results of this chapter.

The text does assume a basic knowledge of mathematics and some familiarity with conventional computing, but no more than that. The book should in fact be of value to *anyone* interested in applying neural network techniques to real-world problems – from the engineer or information technologist to the technical manager.

1.3   A brief overview

As argued above, the proper use of neural networks needs to be grounded within a mathematical framework. Statistical pattern recognition provides the most useful theoretical framework and neural networks are therefore presented from this perspective in Chapter 2. The original approach to neural networks[2], however, was mostly from a geometrical perspective and this is reflected in the order in which the material is presented. The chapter concentrates on the three types of neural networks most commonly used as knowledge of these is sufficient to tackle nearly all of the applications likely to be of interest. Chapter 3 is all about the management of neural computing projects and it is therefore suggested that managers might want to read through Chapter 2 fairly quickly before having a detailed look at Chapter 3; vice versa for the engineers and computer scientists!

Everyone should then be back on track by Chapter 4 which is essential to decide whether or not the application under consideration lends itself to the neural computing approach. The issue of hardware versus software is no longer a controversial one when implementing neural network solutions and this is reflected by the fact that Chapter 5, which deals with this issue, is the shortest chapter in the book. By contrast, a proper understanding of what is required to collect and prepare data for neural computing applications is of paramount importance (Chapter 6). Chapter 7 provides a detailed introduction to the design, training and testing of a prototype neural network, from the encoding of the information to the selection of the network architecture and finally its proper evaluation on the correct type of data set.

The principles introduced in this chapter are put into practice in Chapter 8, in which the reader is taken through two case studies from design and benchmarking to arriving at an optimal solution (known with confidence to be optimal). The level of detail in which these case studies are presented is not available in other texts and should ensure that readers are capable of reproducing similar results on their own problems, whether or not they are using commercially available software packages or writing their own code.

The techniques described in this book and used in Chapter 8 are sufficient for solving real-world problems with neural networks. If, by the end of the book, the reader is interested in delving into alternative techniques or recent theoretical developments, then Chapter 9 is designed to give a brief introduction to these.

1.4   Acknowledgements

The genesis of this book dates back to the end of 1994 when the author was asked to review the Department of Trade and Industry's *Best Practice Guidelines for*

---

[2]From the 1940s to the 1980s.

Developing Neural Computing Applications. Discussions involving both the DTI and the Neural Computing Applications Forum (NCAF) were held during 1995, and Edward Arnold commissioned this book at the end of the 1996 summer. It had become clear, by then, that an almost entirely new book was required and, although there are still sections in the book that draw heavily on the DTI *Best Practice Guidelines* (mostly in Chapter 3), the text is essentially new and is the distillation of the author's experience over the last seven or eight years. That is not to say that others have not made an important contribution to improving the book: the author is especially grateful to the two Research Assistants, Dr James Pardey and Dr Neil Townsend, who carried out the case studies under his guidance; to Drs Peter Cowley and Tom Harris, respectively Chairman and Treasurer of NCAF, for their forbearance; finally, not least to Ian Nabney, Iain Strachan, Graham Hesketh and Simon Cumming, who all made numerous perceptive comments when asked to review the draft within a near-imposssible timescale.

2
MATHEMATICAL BACKGROUND FOR NEURAL COMPUTING

2.1 Introduction

Much hype still surrounds the subject of neural networks, and they are still occasionally described as 'computers that think'. Describing the technology this way leads to unrealistic expectations and discredits an important and valuable engineering tool. Neural networks are not, nor will they ever be, a 'black-box' solution into which data can be poured in the expectation that an answer will emerge. Indeed the success of a neural network application will often depend on how much knowledge about the problem domain can be incorporated into the design and training of the neural network.

This chapter provides an introduction to the most popular types of neural networks, those on which this book will concentrate primarily: Multi-Layer Perceptrons (MLPs), Radial-Basis Function (RBF) networks and Kohonen's Feature Map, sometimes also known as Kohonen's Self-Organising Map. The amount of theory is deliberately kept to a minimum and the reader should refer to the text books and technical papers in the list of references at the end of the book if a more in-depth theoretical treatment is required (in particular, the books by Bishop, 1995, and Ripley, 1996).

2.2 Why neural networks?

In computing terms, neural networks have a unique set of characteristics. They are not programmed, instead they are trained by being repeatedly shown large numbers of examples for the problem under consideration. As a result of this, they can provide good results in relatively short timescales – but only for certain types of problem, and then only when a great deal of care is taken over the collection of the data, the pre-processing of this data and the design of the network.

The key attributes of neural networks can be summarised as follows:

- **learning from experience**: neural networks are particularly suited to problems whose solution is complex and difficult to specify, but which provide an abundance of data from which a response can be learnt (see next section for a definition of learning);

- **generalising from examples**: a vital attribute of any practical self-learning system is the ability to interpolate from a previous learning 'experience'. With careful design, a neural network can be trained to give the correct response to data that it has not previously encountered (and this is often described as the ability to *generalise* on test data);

- **developing solutions faster, and with less reliance on domain expertise**: neural networks learn by example, and as long as examples are available and an appropriate design is adopted, effective solutions can be constructed far more quickly than is possible using traditional approaches, which are entirely reliant on experience in a particular field. However, neural networks are not wholly independent of domain expertise which can be invaluable in choosing the optimal neural network design;

- **computational efficiency**: training a neural network is computationally intensive, but the computational requirements of a fully trained neural network when it is used on test data can be modest. For very large problems, speed can be gained through parallel processing, as neural networks are intrinsically parallel structures;

- **non-linearity**: many other processing techniques are based on the theory of linear systems. In contrast, neural networks can be trained to generate non-linear mappings and this often gives them an advantage for dealing with complex, real-world problems.

2.3   Brief historical background

There are many starting points from which one may begin to try and understand the concepts underlying neural networks. Perhaps the most natural perspective is a historical one and this is the one adopted in this chapter, although it will become obvious that the theoretical framework will gradually shift from geometry and decision boundaries (as in the early days) to statistical pattern recognition.

Artificial neurons as information processing devices were first proposed more than fifty years ago (W.S. McCulloch and W. Pitts: 'A logical calculus of the ideas immanent in nervous activity', *Bulletin of Mathematical Biology*, **5**, 115–133, 1943). Following this early work, the pattern recognition capabilities of *perceptrons*, in which the neurons are arranged in layers, were investigated both theoretically and experimentally throughout the 1950s by Rosenblatt and others, mainly in the US. As shown in Figure 2.1, a neuron computes a weighted summation of its n inputs, the result of which is then thresholded to give a binary output y which is either $+1$ or -1. The neuron assigns input patterns, represented by the vector of numbers $x = (x_1, x_2, \ldots, x_n)$, either to class A (for

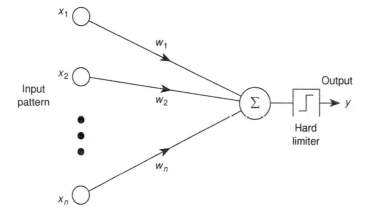

Fig. 2.1 *Schematic diagram of an artificial neuron.*

which y would be 1) or class B (for which y would be -1). Thus:

$$y = f_h\left(\sum_{i=1}^{n} w_i x_i\right) \qquad (2.1)$$

where y is the neuron output (± 1) and f_h is a hard-limiting or threshold function, sometimes known as the neuron's *activation* function, which gives an output of $+1$ whenever $\sum w_i x_i$ is greater than zero (the threshold value) or -1 whenever $\sum w_i x_i$ is less than (or equal to) zero.

Learning consists of adjusting the w_i weights so that the neuron performs the classification task correctly (or as close as possible to it). Multi-class problems can also be solved by having a number of neurons operating in parallel (one per class).

By analogy with neurobiology, the w_i weights are known as *synaptic weights*. This model, however, represents a gross over-simplification of biological neural networks. The simple model of Figure 2.1 does not capture any of the spatio-temporal properties which are known to play a very important role in neurobiological processing. The perceptron model, and its limitations, are discussed further in Section 2.6.

The use of the word 'learning' as a description for the weight adaptation process can be slightly misleading as it may convey the idea of a strong association with the process of human, or animal, learning. In the context of neural networks, learning is usually equivalent to the minimisation of a cost function, such as the mean square error at the output of the network. For this process to converge to an acceptable minimum, very small weight changes are required over large numbers of iterations, a process which bears no resemblance at all to learning in biological systems. With the latter, synaptic modification can only take place with very limited precision (3 bits is the current estimate) and the number of areas within the brain which have plastic (i.e. modifiable) synapses is a matter of considerable debate.

2.4 Pattern recognition

In the 1950s, perceptrons proved themselves adept at learning simple tasks in pattern recognition, but it was shown in the late 1960s that a single layer of perceptrons could not learn how to compute the parity of a binary input pattern (also known as the Exclusive-OR problem). Thus, the perceptron of Figure 2.1 cannot be trained to give an output of, say, $+1$ whenever there is an odd number of 1s in its input binary pattern $x_1, x_2, \ldots, x_n$ (where x_i can either be 1 or 0) and an output of -1 whenever there is an even number of 1s in the input binary pattern (or vice versa). It was recognised, however, that the problem could be solved by having several perceptrons operating in parallel, the outputs of which would become the inputs to another perceptron, i.e. by adding a second layer to the network and creating a *multi-layer perceptron*. The problem was that no learning rule existed for multi-layer networks. This stalled the development of neural networks for more than a decade before a learning algorithm was discovered. As a result, neural networks have now become firmly established over the last ten years, although an important contributory factor has also been the advances in computer power since the 1960s.

The solution to a pattern recognition problem initially involves the collection of a database of *training patterns*. If these patterns have labels associated with them (typically the class of the input pattern), a *supervised* learning procedure is used to train the neural networks. The weights are adapted so as to create a mapping from input patterns to output values, such that the latter approximate the desired values (also known as the *target* values) as closely as possible over the whole training set. The recognition performance of the trained network is then evaluated on *test data*, i.e. patterns which were *not* part of the training database. If the network is able to recognise a large proportion of these new patterns correctly, then it is said to be capable of *generalisation* (a term borrowed from psychology). The aim is to achieve the best possible generalisation performance, given the available training database.

2.5 Pattern classification

In this book, we will concentrate primarily on pattern *classification*, which is the most common type of pattern recognition problem. For example, we might want to decide, on the basis of an X-ray image of the breast, whether someone is in the early stages of breast cancer or not. In this instance, we might want to assign the breast tissue from various regions in the image to one of four possible categories: fat, fibre, benign cyst or cancerous tumour. The other two main uses of neural networks are for *regression* (the prediction of the value of a continuous variable y from an input vector x)[1] and *time-series prediction*. Nearly all that is written about pattern classification in this book would also apply to regression problems (which are discussed in much more detail in Bishop, 1995). Time-series prediction, in which a network is trained to predict the $(n + 1)$th sample in a time series from the previous n samples, is a special case of a regression problem but one which assumes that the underlying data generator is stationary (i.e. its statistical properties are time-independent). For many real-world time series, this assumption does not necessarily hold and more complex learning strategies than those described here are required (see, for example, Lowe and McLachlan, 1995).

2.6 The single-layer perceptron

The perceptron was originally designed as a pattern classifier from a geometrical perspective. Imagine a two-class problem in which the variables for the two classes have very different sets of values. One way to classify the input patterns, if they were two-dimensional patterns, would be to find a separating line[2] such that the patterns, i.e. the (x_1, x_2) values, for one class (class A, say) would all lie to one side of the line and all the patterns for the other class (class B) to the other side of the line. For patterns of class A, we might require the output of the classifier (the perceptron) to be equal to $+1$; for class B patterns, we would then require it to be -1.

Figure 2.2 shows an implementation of such a perceptron with n (rather than 2) inputs in this case. The only difference between this perceptron and that of Figure 2.1 is that we have introduced an extra weight w_0 whose input is fixed at $+1$; this *bias weight* is adaptive like the others and its use allows greater flexibility over the position of the separating line.

The output y of the perceptron is given by:

$$y = f_h\left(\sum_{i=0}^{n} w_i x_i\right) = f_h\left(\sum_{i=1}^{n} w_i x_i + w_0\right) \quad \text{since } x_0 = +1 \quad (2.2)$$

The aim of learning is to find a set of weights w_i such that:

$$y = +1 \text{ for all class A patterns}$$
$$y = -1 \text{ for all class B patterns}$$

Error minimisation

In order to arrive at a weight set which solves the problem, we use error feedback to adjust the weights during training. The idea is to measure an error E at the

---

[1] For example, the quality of a chemical product y based on measurements $(x_1, x_2, \ldots, x_n)$ taken at the end of the manufacturing process.

[2] A plane for a 3-D problem, a hyperplane in higher dimensions.

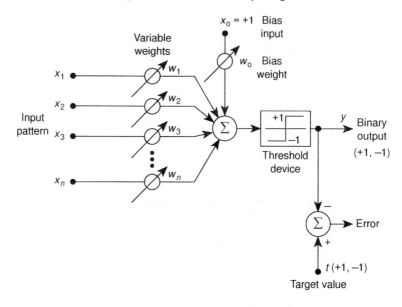

Fig. 2.2 *Single-layer perceptron with bias weight w_0.*

output of the network and then to minimise E by *gradient descent*. We start with an arbitrarily chosen weight vector $\mathbf{w}^0$ and compute the gradient of the error with respect to each weight, i.e. $\partial E / \partial w_i$ for weight w_i. The next vector $\mathbf{w}^1$ is obtained by moving a small distance in the direction of steepest descent, i.e. along the negative of the gradient. For an individual weight w_i in the weight vector $\mathbf{w}$, the weight update Δw_i (i.e. the change in weight from the current weight to the new weight) is given by:

$$\Delta w_i = -\eta \frac{\partial E}{\partial w_i} \tag{2.3}$$

where η is a small parameter which sets the step size (usually called the *learning rate*). Learning is an iterative process whereby all the patterns in the training set are presented in turn, several times, at the input to the network and Equation (2.3) is applied to each weight, for each pattern presentation. Very small changes of weight are repeatedly made until a set of weights is obtained which minimises the error function E over all the patterns in the training set. The choice of the value for η is critical; if it is too large, the error-correction process can overshoot and divergent oscillations may occur. If it is too low, then the weights take a very long time to converge.

The perceptron learning rule

Let the target value t be $+1$ if the input pattern belongs to class A, and let t be -1 if the pattern belongs to class B. If the perceptron correctly classifies a pattern from class A, we will have:

$$y = f_h\left(\sum w_i x_i\right) = t = +1$$

In other words, $\sum w_i x_i > 0$. Similarly, if the perceptron correctly classifies a pattern from class B, we will have:

$$y = f_h \sum(w_i x_i) = t = -1$$

In this case, $\sum w_i x_i < 0$. It is easier to express this in vector form as follows:

For vectors from class A, we want $w^T x > 0$

For vectors from class B, we want $w^T x < 0$

where w^T is the transpose of w. The perceptron makes its decision on the *sign* of $w^T x$; for all input patterns, we want $w^T (xt) > 0$. This allows us to define the following error function, which is known as the perceptron criterion:

$$E = -\sum_{x \in \mathcal{M}} w^T (xt) \qquad (2.4)$$

where $\mathcal{M}$ is the set of input patterns x which are misclassified by the current weight set w (if no patterns are misclassified, $E = 0$).

If we use gradient descent, as in Equation (2.3), with the perceptron criterion, we obtain

$$\Delta w_i = \eta x_i^p t^p \qquad (2.5)$$

for the pth pattern in the training set (assuming, of course, that pattern p belongs to $\mathcal{M}$), since $\partial E / \partial w_i = -x_i t$. Equation (2.5) is known as the *perceptron learning rule*. It is applied to each weight in turn, including the bias weight, before the next pattern x^{p+1} is presented to the perceptron. For any data set which is linearly separable, it can be guaranteed to find a solution in a finite number of steps. In general, the solution will not be unique and will depend on the choice of the initial values for w_i.

If the classes are *not* linearly separable, the perceptron learning rule does *not* converge and the decision boundary oscillates between a number of positions. Consider the previously mentioned parity problem, which requires binary input vectors to be classified as class A if they have an odd number of 1s, and as class B otherwise. For the two-dimensional version of this problem, the input patterns $x = (0, 1)$ and $(1, 0)$ belong to class A while the input patterns $x = (0, 0)$ and $(1, 1)$ belong to class B, and there is clearly no single straight line which can separate the two classes.

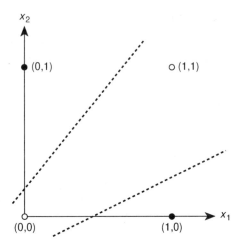

Fig. 2.3 *The Exclusive-OR problem.*

We have already mentioned earlier on in this chapter that the inability of the perceptron learning rule to cope with data sets which are not linearly separable received much attention at the end of the 1960s, to the detriment of the cause of neural networks in general. A possible solution to the Exclusive-OR problem, however, is shown in Figure 2.4 and would be known to any first-year electronic engineering undergraduate. The outputs of the OR gate and the NAND gate (both of which can be implemented by a perceptron), in the *first* layer, act as inputs to an AND gate (another perceptron) in the *second* layer. Thus the Exclusive-OR function *can* be computed with a multi-layer architecture and this was indeed recognised in the late 1960s as a way round the shortcomings of single-layer perceptrons. No further progress was possible at that time, however, because no learning rule then existed for adjusting the weights of the first layer on the basis of the error at the output of the second layer.

2.7 From the 1960s to today: multi-layer networks

The Exclusive-OR problem is, in many ways, a false problem, as we will now explain. (It is regrettable that it is still used occasionally as a toy problem for testing neural network software.) All the emphasis up to the end of the 1960s was on the implementation of Boolean logic functions, which require the decision boundaries to discriminate perfectly between the different classes. The emphasis of the last decade has been completely different: it is now generally accepted that the strength of neural networks lies in their ability to analyse and recognise complex patterns in real-world data. There is one characteristic

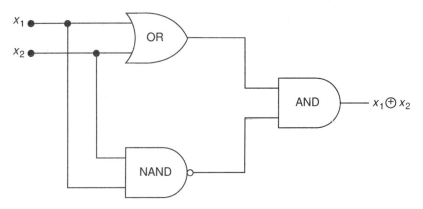

Fig. 2.4 *A possible solution to the Exclusive-OR problem.*

of real-world data which dominates all others: it is intrinsically noisy. With real-world data sets, it is *not* possible to classify all of the data correctly; there will always be regions of overlap in input space such that some of the patterns will end up on the wrong side of the decision boundary. In such a context, the perceptron criterion no longer makes sense and we introduce instead a sum-of-squares error function:

$$E = \frac{1}{2} \sum_{p=1}^{P} (y^p - t^p)^2$$

where y^p is the (single) output of the multi-layer network for pattern p and t^p is the corresponding target value (0 or 1 for a classification problem, the desired value for a regression problem). Minimisation of the error function E will give rise to a set of network weights such that the squared error between the output of the network and the corresponding target value is minimised over all patterns P in the training set. In order to minimise E using gradient descent, we need to be able to differentiate it with respect to *every* weight in the network. This is clearly not possible if we retain the hard-limiting non-linearities of the single-layer perceptron. They are therefore replaced by *continuous differentiable functions* which are linear for small inputs and saturate for large inputs (positive or negative). The most popular such function is the sigmoid function which is shown in Figure 2.5.

We will show in the next section that the use of a squared error criterion at the output of the network together with sigmoid non-linearities for the neurons provides the basis of the learning algorithm for multi-layer perceptrons.

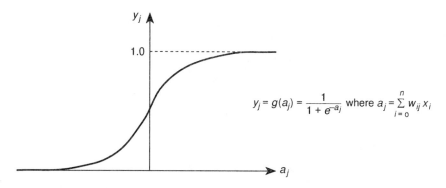

$$y_j = g(a_j) = \frac{1}{1 + e^{-a_j}} \quad \text{where } a_j = \sum_{i=0}^{n} w_{ij} x_i$$

Fig. 2.5 *The sigmoid activation function for the jth neuron in an MLP.*

2.8 Multi-layer perceptrons and the error back-propagation algorithm

Figure 2.6 is a schematic diagram for an *I-J-K* (two-layer) perceptron, for which $I = 5$ (five input parameters), $J = 3$ (three hidden units) and $K = 3$ (three output classes). Note that the bias weights to the hidden units, w_{0j}, and to the output units, w_{0k}, are not shown on this diagram. As before, the bias weights represent an extra weight for each unit whose input is fixed at 1.0 but whose value is otherwise adjusted in exactly the same way as the other weights in the network. Note also that this is a *two-layer* perceptron, because we consider layers of weights, not layers of units. (This is in contrast with many other texts or software packages in which the MLP of Figure 2.6 would be referred to as a three-layer MLP. The problem with referring to layers of units is that it produces an ambiguous nomenclature, with a direct transition from the single-layer perceptron of Figure 2.2 to the 'three-layer' architecture of Figure 2.6.)

For a *K*-class problem, we need *K* output units instead of just the single unit required for a 2-class problem. The error function therefore becomes:

$$E = \frac{1}{2} \sum_{p=1}^{P} \sum_{k=1}^{K} (y_k^p - t_k^p)^2 = \frac{1}{2} \sum_p \sum_k \left(g \sum_j w_{jk} y_j^p - t_k^p \right)^2 \quad (2.6)$$

since $y_k = g(a_k) = g(\sum w_{jk} y_j)$. Similarly, since $y_j = g(a_j) = g(\sum w_{ij} x_i)$, we can now expand Equation (2.6) as follows:

$$E = \frac{1}{2} \sum_p \sum_k \left(g \sum_j w_{jk} g \left(\sum_i w_{ij} x_i^p \right) - t_k^p \right)^2 \quad (2.7)$$

Equation (2.7) may appear daunting at first sight. The only reason for including it here, however, is to demonstrate that *E* is now a continuous differentiable

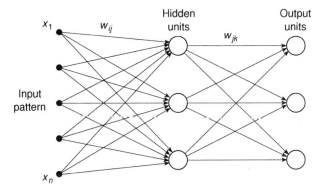

Fig. 2.6 *5-3-3 multi-layer perceptron (bias weights are not shown).*

function of *every* weight since g, the sigmoid activation function of Figure 2.5, can be differentiated. The calculation of the gradient of the error function with respect to each weight in the network (i.e. the $\partial E / \partial w_{ij}$ or $\partial E / \partial w_{jk}$ terms) only requires the application of the chain rule and a knowledge of mathematics equivalent to that of a first-year undergraduate on a science or engineering degree course. This gives rise to the *error back-propagation algorithm* (which is derived formally in Appendix A) for updating the weights in a multi-layer perceptron. For the two-layer architecture which we have been using throughout this section, Appendix A shows that we end up with the following weight update equations:

For the hidden-to-output layer weights:

$$\Delta w_{jk} = -\eta \frac{\partial E}{\partial w_{jk}} = -\eta \delta_k y_j \tag{2.8}$$

$$\text{where } \delta_k = \frac{\partial E}{\partial a_k} = (y_k - t_k) y_k (1 - y_k) \tag{2.9}$$

For the input-to-hidden layer weights:

$$\Delta w_{ij} = -\eta \frac{\partial E}{\partial w_{ij}} = -\eta \delta_j y_i \tag{2.10}$$

$$\text{where } \delta_j = \frac{\partial E}{\partial a_j} = \sum_k \delta_k w_{jk} y_j (1 - y_j) \tag{2.11}$$

The forms of Equations (2.8) and (2.10) are identical, the only difference between the two equations being in the definition of the δs in Equations (2.9) and (2.11). The δ_j for a hidden unit depends on the δ_ks of all the output units to which it is connected via its w_{jk} weights. Thus the minimisation of E using gradient descent requires the propagation of errors (δs) backwards and this gives rise to the name of the algorithm.

Note that convergence is sometimes faster if a 'momentum term' is added to Equations (2.8) and (2.10). Thus:

$$\Delta w_{jk} = w_{jk}(\tau + 1) - w_{jk}(\tau) = -\eta \delta_k y_j + \alpha(w_{jk}(\tau) - w_{jk}(\tau - 1)) \quad (2.12)$$
$$\Delta w_{ij} = w_{ij}(\tau + 1) - w_{ij}(\tau) = -\eta \delta_j y_i + \alpha(w_{ij}(\tau) - w_{ij}(\tau - 1)) \quad (2.13)$$

where $0 < \alpha < 1.0$ and τ is the iteration number. (A Greek symbol has been chosen rather than the more usual t because the latter indicates the target value throughout this chapter.)

The end of the next section discusses briefly how these equations are applied to update the weights during the training of an MLP. The issue is then considered in more detail in Chapter 7, in particular in Section 7.7 on the training and testing of a prototype multi-layer network.

2.9 Training a multi-layer perceptron

Choice of architecture

In nearly all applications of neural network classifiers, we are interested in the generalisation performance of the trained network on a test set of previously unseen input patterns. We therefore need to choose the network architecture which will give the best generalisation performance for a given set of input variables. It has been shown (Cybenko, 1989; Hornik *et al.*, 1989) that a two-layer MLP with sigmoid non-linearities can approximate any function with arbitrary accuracy and this therefore reduces the problem of defining the network architecture to one of choosing the number of hidden units. This is an issue of *model order selection* and depends on the complexity of the underlying function which the MLP is approximating. Too many hidden units and *over-fitting* will occur. As shown in Figure 2.7, a curve fitted with too many parameters follows all the small details or noise but gives very poor interpolation on the test set. Similarly, an MLP with too many hidden units will generalise very badly.

The use of training, validation and test sets

The number of inputs I in an I-j-K MLP is determined by the number of features or input parameters available for the problem under consideration. The number of outputs K is equal to the number of classes (although a two-class problem only requires a single output unit, since class B is simply 'not class A').

Training therefore consists in determining the optimal number j of hidden units together with the corresponding set of w_{ij} weights in the first layer and w_{jk} weights in the second layer. For every value of j considered during this search, at least ten different I-j-K networks should be trained. This means that ten networks with exactly the same architecture should be trained, but with a different set of initial weights in each case. The initial weights should always be

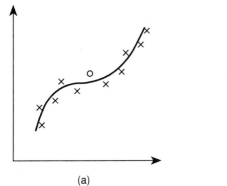
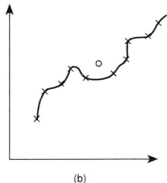

(a)   (b)

Fig. 2.7 *(a) A good fit to noisy data (b) Over-fitting. (× = training set, ○ = test pattern.)*

small random values near zero (both positive and negative) so that the initial values of the y_js and of the y_ks are all close to 0.5 (corresponding to the middle of the approximately linear part of the sigmoid function). Note that it may also be necessary to carry out a search to discover the optimal value of η and α although these should principally affect the learning time rather than the generalisation performance. For most problems, reasonable values for η and α are between 0.01 and 0.1, and 0.5 respectively.

The available data should be partitioned (evenly if possible) into three data sets: the training set, the validation set and the test set. The training set represents the input–output information (i.e. a set of input features/parameters and the associated class labels) which is used to modify the w_{ij} and w_{jk} weights according to the learning rule (i.e. Equations (2.8) and (2.10) or (2.12) and (2.13) if momentum is being used). The set of patterns in the training set is repeatedly presented in random order to the network and the weight update equations are usually applied after the presentation of each pattern. When all the patterns have been presented once to the network, one *epoch* of training is set to have taken place. It may take hundreds of epochs for learning to occur. The question therefore arises: when is the learning process completed? This is where the validation set comes into play.

The validation set is used *purely to decide when to stop training*, not for weight update. A network which is over-trained will learn the details of the training data rather than the underlying input–output mapping and is therefore likely to perform poorly when given new data which it has not previously seen (the test set). The training process is monitored by keeping a close watch on the classification error *on the validation set*. When this stops decreasing or even starts to rise, training should stop. Hence the stopping criterion should be the point at which the minimum classification error on the validation set is reached. At this point, the network's weights are 'frozen' and the generalisation performance is assessed on previously unseen data, namely the test set[3]. The issues of stopping criterion and selection of an 'optimal network' are discussed again in much more detail in Chapter 7.

If it is not possible to split the available data equally between training, validation and test sets (usually because of lack of data), more complicated cross-validation techniques can be employed. A simple variant of such a technique is described for one of the Case Studies in Chapter 8 which does suffer from shortage of data.

2.10 Probabilistic interpretation of network outputs

The point was made in Section 2.6 that the strength of multi-layer networks lies in their ability to recognise complex patterns in real-world data which is intrinsically noisy or uncertain. The calculus of uncertainty is probability and we can use it to our advantage by operating neural networks within a probabilistic framework. In this section, we show how the outputs of a neural network classifier, under the right conditions, estimate the *probability* of an input pattern belonging to a given class. In a two-class problem, the single output will vary between 0 (class A, say) and 1.0 (class B). If the output is close to 0.5, then we know that the input pattern lies close to the decision boundary and there is therefore some uncertainty as to its classification.

Consider again a classification problem with K output classes. Bayes' theorem states that

$$P(C_k \mid x) = \frac{p(x \mid C_k)\,P(C_k)}{p(x)} \tag{2.14}$$

The left-hand side $P(C_k \mid x)$ is known as the *posterior* probability that the class is C_k given that the input vector is x. On the right-hand side of the equation, the quantity $p(x \mid C_k)$ is known as the class conditional probability or the *likelihood* of x for the given class C_k. The likelihood is multiplied by the other quantity in the numerator, the *prior* probability, $P(C_k)$. If the data in the training set can be assumed to have been generated in a way which is typical of the way in which the test data will also be collected, then we can estimate the prior probabilities by simply calculating the fractions of the training set which belong to each class.

The denominator, $p(x)$, is in effect a normalisation factor which ensures that the posterior probabilities sum to 1.0. It can be shown (see, for example, Bishop (1995)) that:

$$p(x) = \sum_{k=1}^{K} p(x \mid C_k) P(C_k)$$

---

[3]Note that the terms 'validation set' and 'test set' are sometimes used in the opposite sense in some texts or software packages. This causes unnecessary confusion; the test set should always be the data set on which the generalisation performance of a trained network is tested.

The Bayes *decision rule* states that the probability of misclassification is minimised when we make the following decision:

Assign x to class C_i if $P(C_i \mid x) > P(C_j \mid x)$ for all $j \neq i$.

In traditional statistical pattern recognition, the posterior probabilities are computed by evaluating the *right-hand side* of Equation (2.14). As already explained, the prior probabilities $P(C_k)$ can be estimated from the proportions of the training examples which belong to each class. The estimation of $p(x \mid C_k)$, however, is not as straightforward. Broadly, there are two types of methods:

1. make a strong assumption about the form of the conditional density function for the problem under consideration; this usually turns out to mean that $p(x \mid C_k)$ is modelled as a multivariate normal, or Gaussian, density function. The use of the Gaussian assumption leads to quadratic discriminants, or linear discriminants if one further assumption[4] is made about the distribution of the data within the K classes (see Bishop (1995) or James (1985));

2. estimate $p(x \mid C_i)$ using *non-parametric* methods. This eventually leads to nearest-neighbour classification techniques.

In a key paper, Richard and Lippmann (1991) showed that neural networks estimate the posterior probability $P(C_k \mid x)$ directly. There are two requirements for this to hold: a 1-out-of-K output coding (so that $t_k = 1$ if x belongs to C_k and 0 otherwise) must be used and the network weights must be chosen so as to minimise a squared-error cost function[5]. Since this has been part of the standard assumptions in this chapter, we have the key result that, under these conditions, network outputs are estimates of posterior probabilities. This is an important result which has established neural computing as a principled method within the framework of statistical pattern recognition.

2.11 Unsupervised learning—the motivation

Up to now, we have assumed that all the data samples available to us have been *labelled* to show the class to which they belong. The classification procedures which we have considered are described as *supervised* since the correct answer must be presented to the network during training.

For many real-world problems, the database of sample patterns will *not* have all the examples labelled. The collection and labelling of a large number of samples is a costly and time-consuming exercise. Often, a small proportion of the total number of patterns will have been assigned membership of a class but the great majority of the sample patterns will have no labels associated with

---

[4]That of equal covariance matrices for all classes.

[5]Strictly speaking, for a multi-class problem, the cross-entropy error function should be used and the output units should have a *softmax* activation function—see Bishop (1995), pages 230 to 240.

them. In other cases, it may be valuable, at the beginning of an investigation, to gain some insight into the nature of the data without making any *a priori* assumptions. The discovery of distinct sub-classes or major departures from expected characteristics may significantly alter the approach to designing the classifier. Finally, there may be problems for which there is no knowledge of the classes or categories which may exist within the data and the whole database is simply a collection of unlabelled patterns.

Is there anything that we can learn in the absence of labelled data? The answer is a qualified yes – the attempt to discover any underlying structure in the data is known as *cluster analysis* (or clustering), which is a form of *unsupervised* learning. The qualification arises from the fact that any clustering technique relies on a number of assumptions which have to be made about the data, some of which may be problem dependent.

2.12   Cluster analysis

A cluster is comprised of a number of *similar* input vectors grouped together. If there are n features used to describe the data, a cluster can be described as a region in n-dimensional space containing a relatively *high density* of points, separated from other such regions by regions containing a relatively low density of points.

This is a simple definition but the problem of deciding how many clusters exist in a data set is a non-trivial one. The key issue in identifying clusters is the specification of a *similarity* measure. The most obvious measure of similarity between two patterns (or, strictly speaking, dissimilarity) is the distance between them. A simple form of cluster analysis might involve computing the matrix of distances between all pairs of patterns in the data set. The distance between patterns in the same cluster should then be much less than the distance between patterns in different clusters.

Euclidean distance is by far the most regularly used metric. However, it implicitly assigns more weight to parameters or features with large ranges than those with small ranges. Suppose that two parameters in a weather prediction system are the pressure p which might vary from 900 to 1100 millibars and the temperature T which is given a range from $-10\,°C$ to $30\,°C$. The Euclidean distance $d(i, k)$ between two input vectors $(p_i\ T_i)$ and $(p_k\ T_k)$ will depend principally on the pressure difference rather than the temperature difference because the former has a dynamic range which is five times greater.

In order to prevent features from dominating Euclidean distance calculations simply because they have large numerical values, the feature values are often *normalised* to have zero mean and unit variance over all P patterns. Thus for the jth feature, its mean μ_j and its variance σ_j^2 are first computed:

$$\mu_j = \frac{1}{P} \sum_{i=1}^{P} x_{ij} \quad \text{and} \quad \sigma_j^2 = \frac{1}{P-1} \sum_{i=1}^{P} (x_{ij} - \mu_j)^2$$

Then we have:

$$x_{ij}^* = \frac{x_{ij} - \mu_j}{\sigma_j}$$

where x_{ij}^* is the normalised value of x_{ij}.

2.13 Clustering algorithms

The objective of any clustering algorithm can now be defined as follows:

> *Given P patterns in n-dimensional space, find a partition of the patterns into K groups, or clusters, such that the patterns in a cluster are more similar to each other than to patterns in different clusters.*

The solution to this problem may at first sight appear to be relatively straightforward. We define a criterion function (based on the squared Euclidean distance, for example) that measures the clustering quality of any partition of the data, evaluate it for all possible partitions containing K clusters and choose the partition which optimises the criterion. Unfortunately, there are approximately $K^P/K!$ ways of partitioning P patterns into K clusters; for example, there are 34 105 distinct partitions of 10 patterns into 4 clusters and approximately 1.1×10^{10} partitions of just 19 patterns also into 4 clusters.

To avoid this combinatorial explosion, the criterion function should only be evaluated for a small number of candidate partitions. The approach most frequently used to find near-optimal partitions is again iterative optimisation. Starting from an initial partition, the patterns are moved from one cluster to another if such a move will improve the value of the criterion function. Each successive partition is a perturbation of the previous one and, therefore, only a few partitions are considered. Of course, this approach can only guarantee local rather than global optimisation.

Clustering criterion

The most common clustering strategy is based on the minimisation of a square-error criterion. Suppose that the P patterns in the data set are partitioned into K clusters $\{C_1, C_2, \ldots, C_K\}$ such that cluster C_k has p_k patterns and each pattern is in one cluster only, so that

$$\sum_{k=1}^{K} p_k = P$$

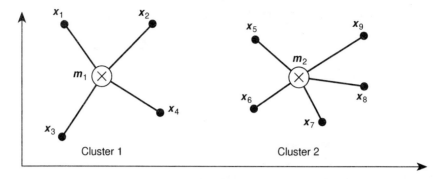

Fig. 2.8 *Square-error clustering for simple 2-D data set* $(P = 9, K = 2)$.

Let each of the K clusters be characterised by a mean vector m_k which is the mean of all the patterns within that cluster. Thus

$$m_k = \frac{1}{p_k} \sum_{x \in C_k} x$$

m_k can be viewed as the most representative pattern within cluster C_k, sometimes known as a *prototype* or *cluster centre*.

The squared error for cluster C_k, e_k^2, is the sum of the squared Euclidean distance between each pattern in C_k and its cluster centre m_k:

$$e_k^2 = \sum_{x \in C_K} (x - m_k)^T (x - m_k) = \sum_{x \in C_k} \|x - m_k\|^2$$

Then the sum of squared errors is defined by:

$$E_K^2 = \sum_{k=1}^K e_k^2 = \sum_{k=1}^K \sum_{x \in C_k} \|x - m_k\|^2 \tag{2.15}$$

Thus the objective of a square-error clustering is to find a partition containing K clusters which minimises E_K^2 for fixed K. E_K^2 measures the total squared error incurred in representing the P patterns $x^1, \ldots, x^P$ by K cluster centres $m_1, \ldots, m_K$. Figure 2.8 shows the cluster centres m_1 and m_2 for a set of P two-dimensional patterns $(P = 9, K = 2)$. For clusters C_1 and C_2, the vectors m_1 and m_2 minimise the sum of the squared lengths of the 'error vectors' $x - m_k$.

K-means clustering algorithm

The K-means algorithm is an example of an iterative clustering algorithm which, for a given value of K, aims to minimise E_K^2, starting from an initial partition of the data set. The algorithm proceeds as follows:

1. Select an initial set of cluster centres $\{m_1, m_2, \ldots, m_K\}$
2. Assign each of the P patterns to its closest cluster centre

   i.e. x belongs to cluster C_i if $\|x - m_i\| < \|x - m_j\|$ for $i \neq j$

3. Compute new cluster centres as the means of the K clusters (this minimises the cost function E_K^2 defined in Equation (2.15))
4. If the position of any cluster centre changes, return to step 2; otherwise, stop.

The above algorithm updates all the cluster centres at once (at the end of step 3), after the P patterns in the data set have been assigned to one of the C_k clusters in step 2, and is known as the *batch K-means* algorithm. The *adaptive* version of the algorithm is a stochastic procedure whereby *one* cluster centre is updated every time a pattern x is chosen at random from the data set. The cluster centre nearest to x has its position updated according to the following rule:

$$m_i^* = m_i + \eta(x - m_i)$$

Thus the cluster centre m_i is moved closer to x (so as to minimise the error vector $x - m_i$) by a small amount dependent on the learning rate η. This procedure is more susceptible to being trapped in poor local minima and the final partitioning depends on the order in which the patterns are presented. However, it is an *on-line* learning algorithm in the sense that it can be used for problems in which the input patterns are acquired sequentially and the clustering has to be done in real time.

The choice of a value for K

The assumption in all of this section has been that the number of clusters is known *a priori*. For a new data set, we cannot make such an assumption and perhaps the most difficult problem in cluster analysis is that of deciding just how many clusters are present. When clustering is done by optimising a criterion function, the usual approach is to repeat the clustering algorithm for $K = 2$, $K = 3$, etc., and see how E_K^2 changes with K. It is obvious that E_K^2 must decrease monotonically with K, since the squared error can be reduced each time K is increased merely by transferring a single pattern to the new cluster. If the P patterns are really grouped into K_{opt} well-separated clusters, E_K^2 should decrease rapidly until $K = K_{opt}$, decreasing much more slowly after that until it reaches zero when $K = P$. Thus one method for identifying the value of K_{opt} is to plot E_K^2 versus K and decide where the 'knee of the curve' is to be found.

2.14 Data visualisation—Kohonen's feature map

It is often useful, before embarking on a comprehensive cluster analysis, to attempt to visualise the data in a lower dimensional space. There are classical algorithms for this (for example, Sammon's mapping (Sammon, 1969)) but in this section we will consider a neural network algorithm for data visualisation (usually in 2-D): Kohonen's feature map (Kohonen, 1982 and 1990) which has its roots in neurobiology and is a form of K-means clustering with an attempt to preserve the structure of the data when constructing the 2-D representation.

Neurobiological background to Kohonen's feature map

The placement of neurons in the sensory pathways of the brain is spatially ordered and often reflects physical characteristics of the stimulus being sensed. For example, nerve cells and fibres in the auditory pathway are arranged anatomically in relation to the *frequency* which causes the greatest response in each neuron. Tactile and visual inputs are also mapped onto different areas of the cerebral cortex in a topologically ordered manner. The neurons therefore transform input signals into a *place-coded probability distribution* of the data by sites of maximum relative activity within the map. The information so coded can then be readily accessed by higher-order processors using relatively simple connection schemes. Although much of the spatial organisation is genetically pre-determined, Kohonen has argued that some of it, especially at the higher levels of processing, is created as a result of learning by modification of synaptic connections.

1-D version of Kohonen's algorithm

Kohonen's *self-organising* algorithm is usually given in its 2-D version, hence the name of feature *map*. It will initially be described here for the 1-D case, as this more clearly shows it to be a form of the adaptive K-means algorithm with topological constraints. Refer also to the description of the K-means algorithm in Section 2.13 when considering the 1-D Kohonen algorithm given here:

1. Select an initial set of K weight vectors $\{m_1, m_2, \ldots, m_K\}$ for each of the K units in the feature map. The weight vectors are of the same dimension as the input patterns x. The units are topologically ordered in a 1-D array as shown in Figure 2.9.
2. Choose a pattern x from the training data set and identify the unit k whose weight vector m_k is nearest to x

   i.e. the one for which $\|x - m_k\| < \|x - m_{k'}\|$ when $k \neq k'$

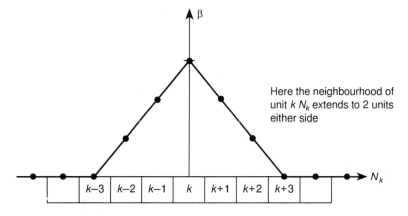

Here the neighbourhood of unit k N_k extends to 2 units either side

| | $k-3$ | $k-2$ | $k-1$ | k | $k+1$ | $k+2$ | $k+3$ | |

Fig. 2.9 *The neighbourhood-dependent gain term β in a 1-D Kohonen array.*

3. (a) Move m_k closer to x by an amount determined by the learning rate η

$$m_k^* = m_k + \eta(x - m_k)$$

(b) Move also other units which are in the *neighbourhood* of m_k in the 1-D array by an amount proportional to β, where β is as shown in Figure 2.9:

$$m_{k\pm p}^* = m_{k\pm p} + \eta\beta(x - m_{k\pm p})$$

Thus units adjacent to unit k will also move closer to x, units further away by smaller amounts ($0 \le p \le 2$ on Figure 2.9);

4. Go back to 2.

Every time that a pre-determined number of passes through all P patterns in the training data set has been completed, decrease the size of the neighbourhood by one unit.

At the start of training, the neighbourhood is such that it covers the entire array. It is then slowly reduced during the initial phase of training (see step 4) and it is during this phase that the topological ordering takes place: similar inputs are mapped to units close to each other in the array, for example k, $k - 1$ and $k + 1$. At the end of this phase, the algorithm reduces to the adaptive K-means algorithm. A secondary training phase then occurs during which fine-tuning of the centre positions is used to decrease E_K^2 further. Note that the learning rate parameter η is usually time-dependent but this has been omitted from the description of the algorithm in order to simplify matters. The neighbourhood function shown in Figure 2.9 is also simpler than that normally used with the 2-D feature map, for which it usually has the shape of a 'Mexican hat' or a 2-D Gaussian.

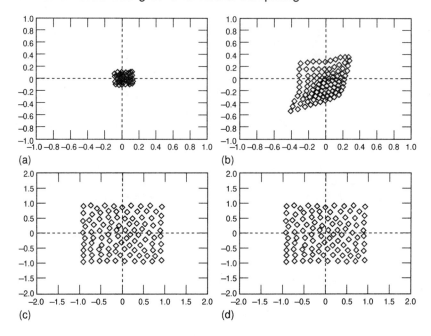

Fig. 2.10 *Weight vectors for 100 units in Kohonen feature map: (a) initial distribution; (b) after 20 iterations; (c) after 40 iterations; (d) after 100 iterations.*

2-D feature map

The most common implementation of Kohonen's feature map is in two dimensions. The description of the algorithm for the 1-D case can be adapted by replacing k everywhere by i, j and using a 2-D neighbourhood defined in terms of Euclidean distances on the map[6]. The self-organising properties of the algorithm can best be demonstrated using a data set of randomly distributed 2-D input vectors. Suppose that there are 10 000 such 2-D vectors uniformly distributed within the area defined by $(-1.0 < x, y < 1.0)$. A 2-D feature map of 100 units (or 'neurons') will consist of a 10×10 grid.

The initial m_k vectors are also given a random distribution $(-0.1 < x, y < 0.1)$ as shown in Figure 2.10(a). After 10 iterations through the training set of 10 000 examples, the distribution of the m_k vectors for the 100 units has begun to spread out and the map starts to form a mesh as shown in Figure 2.10(b). It should be obvious from visual inspection that the (x, y) co-ordinates of the m_k weight vectors are plotted in topologically ordered fashion, i.e. according to their (i, j) position in the 10×10 array of units. After 40 iterations, the

---

[6]Note that the public-domain software made available by Kohonen uses a slightly different definition of neighbourhood and also recommends the use of a hexagonal grid rather than the square grid adopted throughout this book.

distribution of the m_k weight vectors now follows the regular distribution of the 10 000 training points (see Figure 2.10(c)). The positions of the weight vectors are optimised for the last 60 iterations using the adaptive K-means algorithm to give the final distribution of the fully-trained feature map after 100 iterations (Figure 2.10(d)). Note the different scales for Figure 2.10(c) and (d) in comparison to Figure 2.10(a) and (b).

The type of results presented in Figure 2.10 are similar to those given by Kohonen in order to demonstrate the topological ordering properties of the algorithm. These results can be slightly misleading, however, for those who are not familiar with Kohonen's feature map. It should be stressed that, in the real applications of the map as opposed to the toy problem of Figure 2.10, the input data x and hence the weight vectors m_k are *not* two-dimensional but of arbitrary dimension. For a K-unit map, one ends up with K weight vectors which are effectively K prototype vectors distributed amongst the original x vectors according to data density (since Kohonen's algorithm is a clustering algorithm). The advantage of the feature map is that each of these prototype vectors has a meaningful (i, j) index in a 2-D array such that prototype vectors which are close to each other in the original n-dimensional input space will be neighbours in the 2-D array ('topology preservation').

Conclusion

The main goal of Kohonen's self-organising algorithm is to transform input patterns of arbitrary dimension into a two-dimensional feature map with topological ordering. During training, each pattern in the data set is presented to the network, one at a time, in random order. As the spatial ordering progresses during the initial phase of training, each pattern gives rise to a localised region of activity in the feature map against a background of lower activity. Eventually, once the feature map has been trained, the presentation of an input pattern should cause a localised group of units to be active.

2.15   From the feature map to classification

We began the section on clustering analysis by considering the rationale for applying clustering techniques to a pattern recognition problem. In particular, it was stated that clustering might give some insight into the nature of the data and lead to the discovery of distinct sub-classes or major departures from expected characteristics. If, at the end of this phase, a classifier needs to be designed, then there is a very direct extension from the feature map using *vector quantisation*.

The main application of vector quantisation is usually in *data compression* but it will be described here in the context of pattern classification. In this case, there are several m_k prototype vectors assigned to each class (in this context, these are known as *codebook vectors*). Thus the weight, or prototype, vectors m_k of the

100 units of a trained 10×10 feature map could be chosen as the 100 codebook vectors for the data set (with $10\,000$ vectors in the input database, this gives a data compression factor of 100:1). With that many units, it is clear that there will be several codebook vectors per class.

The weight vectors m_k in a trained feature map are a coarse representation of the unconditional probability density function $p(x)$ of the input data. In order to assign class labels to the units of the feature map, which now become the codebook vectors, vectors with known labels are presented at the input to the map and the units are assigned to different classes by majority voting. The classification accuracy is then improved by moving the codebook vectors away from the decision surfaces in order to improve discrimination between classes. Let m_C be the codebook vector closest to x; its position in input space is updated according to the Learning Vector Quantisation (LVQ) algorithm (Kohonen, 1990):

$$m_C^* = m_C + \eta(\tau)(x - m_C) \qquad \text{if } x \text{ is classified correctly}$$
$$m_C^* = m_C - \eta(\tau)(x - m_C) \qquad \text{if } x \text{ is classified incorrectly}$$

where $\eta(\tau)$ is a learning rate parameter which decreases monotonically with time.

2.16 Radial Basis Function networks

The outcome of a clustering procedure is a set of centres which are prototype patterns in input space (i.e. the vector m_k vector can be thought of as the average pattern for the kth cluster). With LVQ, this representation can also be used for classification purposes; if class labels are assigned to the prototypes (or codebooks), a test pattern x is assigned the class of the prototype (or codebook) nearest to it. An alternative approach, which also makes use of prototype patterns, is that adopted with Radial Basis Function networks, which are the subject of this section.

A Radial Basis Function (RBF) network is a two-layer network, the output units of which form a linear combination of the basis functions computed by the hidden units. Whereas the neurons in a multi-layer perceptron compute a non-linear function of the scalar product $w \cdot x$, the activation of the hidden units in an RBF network is determined by the Euclidean distance between x and a set of prototype vectors. A typical RBF network is shown in Figure 2.11 (note that the bias weights to the output units are again not shown).

The first layer's non-linear mapping is constructed using a set of *basis functions* whose centres correspond to the prototype vectors in input space. The basis functions are usually chosen to be unnormalised Gaussians and the output activity of the jth hidden unit is then given by:

$$\phi_j(x) = \exp\left(-\frac{\|x - \mu_j\|^2}{2\sigma_j^2}\right) \qquad (2.16)$$

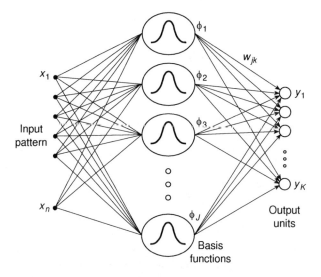

Fig. 2.11 *Architecture of RBF network.*

where x is an n-dimensional input vector, μ_j is the jth prototype vector (corresponding to m_j in Section 2.14) and σ_j is the 'width' of the Gaussian for that prototype or centre. This parameter is chosen so as to ensure that the basis functions give rise to a *localised* response for any input pattern, i.e. they only produce a significant non-zero response when the input pattern belongs to a small localised region of input space close to μ_j. The name 'radial basis function' comes from the fact that the Gaussian functions are radially symmetric: each hidden unit j produces an identical output for input patterns that are found at a fixed radial distance from μ_j.

The Gaussian basis functions are not normalised since their amplitude is effectively set by the weights w_{jk} of the second layer:

$$y_k = \sum_{j=1}^{J} w_{jk}\phi_j + w_{0k} \qquad (2.17)$$

where w_{0k} is the bias weight to output unit k. Thus the output layer forms a weighted linear combination of the hidden unit activations. Hence an RBF network performs a non-linear transformation from $\mathbb{R}^n$, the n-dimensional real-valued input space, to $\mathbb{R}^K$, the K-dimensional real-valued output space, by forming a linear combination of non-linear basis functions. Note that it is also possible to use basis functions which are not Gaussians—see, for example, Lowe (1995) which considers thin plate splines and other non-local basis functions.

2.17 Training an RBF network

One of the main advantages of RBF networks over MLPs is the possibility of setting the free parameters of the hidden units without having to perform a full non-linear optimisation of the network (as with the error back-propagation algorithm). In other words, the training of an RBF network can conveniently be broken down into two independent phases: the selection of the basis functions μ_j and their widths σ_j, followed by learning in the output layer (w_{jk} weights). The former task is typically performed using an unsupervised method, for example the K-means algorithm. For adequate coverage of input space, the number J of basis function centres μ_j *needs to be much greater than the number of clusters in the data.*

The basis function widths σ_j are set once the clustering procedure has been completed. These widths should represent a measure of the spread of the data associated with each μ_j. They will therefore vary according to the data density in different regions of input space, but the over-riding factor is that the basis functions should overlap to some degree in order to give a relatively smooth representation for all training data. This can be achieved, for example, by setting the σ_js to be the average distance between the centres μ_j and the training patterns which belong to that cluster (Hush and Horne, 1993):

$$\sigma_j^2 = \frac{1}{p_j} \sum_{x \in C_j} (x - \mu_j)^T (x - \mu_j) \tag{2.18}$$

where C_j is the set of training patterns grouped with centre μ_j and p_j is the number of patterns in C_j.

Learning in the output layer takes place after all of the above has been completed, i.e. the parameters of the basis functions (μ_j and σ_j) have been determined using only the input data (unsupervised learning). The basis functions are then kept fixed while the output layer weights w_{jk} are obtained in the second, independent, phase of learning which also makes use of the available labels (supervised learning). Since the labelling of data is usually a very time-consuming process, the amount of labelled data is often limited in many applications. In such cases, the two-stage training process of an RBF network presents a real advantage since the non-linear representation of the first layer can be determined using a large quantity of unlabelled data, leaving a relatively small number of parameters in the second (output) layer to be obtained using the labelled data.

Setting the weights in the second layer is a linear optimisation task and can either be done using matrix inversion techniques (Singular Value Decomposition)[7] or iteratively using the Least Mean Square (LMS) algorithm. The use of the latter is very similar to the training of the second layer of a two-layer

---

[7]With Singular Value Decomposition (SVD), the weights are obtained from an eigenvector decomposition of the correlation matrix of the training data from which a pseudo-inverse is calculated (see Press *et al.*, 1992, for further details).

MLP (see Section 2.8), except that the output layer in an RBF network employs linear, rather than sigmoid, units. Thus Equation (2.8) simply becomes:

$$\Delta w_{jk} = -\eta \delta_k y_j \qquad (2.19)$$

$$\text{where } \delta_k = \frac{\partial E}{\partial a_k} = \frac{\partial E}{\partial y_k} \frac{\partial y_k}{\partial a_k} = (y_k - t_k) \qquad (2.20)$$

since $y_k = a_k$ for a linear unit.

The training set consists of input/output pairs (x, t) as before (t is the target output vector), but now the input patterns x are processed by the first layer to generate the $\phi(x)$ values which are then presented to the second layer for the iterative optimisation of the w_{jk} weights using the LMS algorithm. There is no need to use a validation set as with an MLP. The first-layer parameters are determined using unsupervised learning and the second-layer weights w_{jk} using the LMS algorithm which gives a global optimum (linear optimisation). Thus training continues until the mean squared error stops decreasing on the training set at which point the generalisation performance is assessed on the test set.

2.18 Comparison between RBF networks and MLPs

Bishop's book *Neural Networks for Pattern Recognition* (OUP, 1995) has a detailed section comparing the two types of networks. The following is a summary of the key points:

1. RBF networks and MLPs play very similar roles in that they both provide techniques for approximating arbitrary non-linear functional mappings between an input vector x and a set of outputs y.
2. The hidden unit representations of the MLP depend on the weighted linear summation of the inputs, transformed by a sigmoid activation function. By contrast, the hidden units in an RBF network use distance to a prototype vector followed by transformation with a localised function.
3. The MLP forms a *distributed representation* in the space of activation values for the hidden units since, for a given input pattern, many hidden units will typically contribute to the determination of the output value. The representations of the hidden units formed during training must be such that, when combined by the final layer of weights, they generate the correct outputs for a range of possible input values. By contrast, an RBF network with localised basis functions forms a representation in the space of the hidden units which is *local* with respect to the input space because, for a given input pattern, typically only a few hidden units will have significantly non-zero activations.
4. All of the parameters in an MLP are usually determined at the same time as part of a single global training strategy using supervised learning.

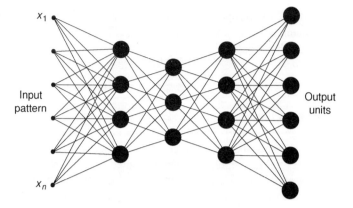

x_1

Input
pattern

Output
units

x_n

Fig. 2.12 *Auto-associative MLP with four layers of weights.*

The correct application of this strategy requires a training set for weight modification, a validation set to decide when to stop training and a test set of previously unseen data to assess generalisation performance. RBF networks only require training and test sets. The training data is used without labels in the first stage of learning and then the same data (or a sub-set of it if not all the input data is labelled) is used to set the weights in the second layer. Since this is a linear optimisation task, there exists a unique minimum for that data set and the chosen centre positions and widths. Hence an RBF network only requires a training and test set fully to characterise its performance.

2.19 Auto-associative neural networks

An auto-associative network, as its name implies, is a network which learns an input–output mapping such that the output is the same as the input (in other words, the target data set is identical to the input data set). There are two main types of auto-associative networks: the Hopfield network (which is covered in the next section) and the auto-associative multi-layer perceptron. An example of the latter is shown in Figure 2.12, where it is apparent that one way to view this architecture is to consider it as two MLPs back to back.

The dimensionality of the input and output is obviously the same and the network is trained, using the error back-propagation algorithm, to generate output vectors y as close as possible to the input vectors x by again minimising the mean squared error over all patterns in the training set:

$$E = \frac{1}{2} \sum_{p=1}^{P} \sum_{k=1}^{K} (y_k^p - x_k^p)^2$$

The key aspect of the auto-associative MLP is that the number of hidden units at the centre of the network is usually chosen to be much smaller than the input/output dimensionality. As a result of this bottleneck, the hidden units extract a low-dimensional representation of the input data and such a network can therefore be used for *data compression*.

It is now clear that four layers of weights (as in Figure 2.12) are required in order to achieve *non-linear* dimensionality reduction (Kramer, 1991; DeMers and Cottrell, 1993). If there are only two layers of weights (as in the standard MLP of Figure 2.6), then the network performs linear principal component analysis[8] whether the hidden units have linear or sigmoid activation functions.

2.20   Recurrent networks

All of the neural networks which we have so far considered are examples of *feedforward* networks, for which the outputs from a set of units are connected only to the inputs of the units in the next layer. A more general type of network is one in which connections are allowed between units *in both directions* (feedback as well as feedforward) and even from a unit to itself (self-feedback). Such a network comes under the generic description of *recurrent* network. There are many types of recurrent networks depending principally on the topology of the network and the way that the feedback is organised. The main application of recurrent networks (except for Hopfield networks) is for processing time-dependent input patterns: for example, in time-series prediction or in learning to recognise time sequences.

The behaviour of recurrent networks is very complex as they are effectively non-linear dynamical systems with feedback and hence they do not necessarily settle down to a stable state even with constant input (Hertz *et al.*, 1991). One important exception to this is the case of networks with symmetric connections (i.e. $w_{ji} = w_{ij}$), a property which is exploited in Hopfield networks.

Hopfield networks are mentioned briefly here primarily for historical reasons. Two papers published by Hopfield in the early 1980s (Hopfield, 1982; Hopfield, 1984) were probably one of the main reasons for the resurgence of interest in neural networks at that time. A Hopfield network is a fully-interconnected feedback network of n neurons with hard-limiting activation functions: the inputs to any one neuron are the weighted outputs from every other neuron. In the original, stochastic model (Hopfield, 1982), each neuron samples its input at random times and changes the value of its output (or not) according to a simple threshold rule:

$$x_j \rightarrow +1 \quad \text{if} \ \sum w_{ij} x_i \geq \theta$$
$$x_j \rightarrow -1 \quad \text{if} \ \sum w_{ij} x_i < \theta$$

---

[8]See Chapter 7 for an explanation of principal component analysis.

where x_i, as before, is the ith element of the input vector x and θ is usually set to zero.

A Hopfield network can be configured to be a *content-addressable memory* for storing binary patterns if the weights w_{ij} are generated using the following rule:

$$w_{ij} = \sum_{p=1}^{P} x_i^p x_j^p$$

for P patterns to be stored in the memory. (Note that the above is a *prescription* rule rather than a learning rule.) Of course, there must be as many neurons in the network as there are bits in the patterns to be stored[9]. On recall, the pattern x is regenerated from its incomplete (or corrupted) version $\hat{x}$ by computing $W\hat{x}$ (where W is the matrix of synaptic weights), thresholding the result according to the threshold rule given above, feeding it back to the input and iterating until the network settles into the stable state x. Hopfield summarises this as follows: *'the content-addressable memory ... correctly yields an entire memory from any subpart of sufficient size'*.

Despite the original enthusiasm for Hopfield networks and the ease with which they can be implemented in silicon integrated circuits (Murray and Tarassenko, 1994), they were never used as content-addressable memories in any real-world applications. It was soon established that the storage capacity of Hopfield networks is extremely poor when compared to conventional content-addressable memories (Tarassenko *et al.*, 1991). If perfect recall is required (i.e. no spurious outputs), then only $n/4 \log_e n$ patterns can be stored – no more than three or four 64-bit patterns, for example. If a probability of recalling the correct pattern of 95% is acceptable (which is most unlikely in real-world applications), the number of patterns which can be stored in the network increases to $0.14n$, still a very low number. Content-addressable memories which are based on the measurement of Hamming distance between the partial or corrupted pattern and the stored memories are simply much more efficient. The Hamming distance between two binary patterns is simply the number of bits which differ between the two patterns; thus $\{0\,0\,1\,0\,1\}$ and $\{1\,0\,1\,0\,0\}$ have a Hamming distance of 2.

The waning interest in Hopfield networks coincided with the re-discovery by Rumelhart *et al.* in 1986 of the error back-propagation algorithm for the training of multi-layer perceptrons. (It is now generally accepted that a very similar algorithm had first been proposed by Werbos in 1974 but it had not been exploited by him or anyone else at the time.) As described earlier on in this chapter, the perceived limitations of single-layer networks could now be overcome and this has led to the application of multi-layer feedforward networks to a wide range of hard pattern recognition problems.

---

[9] If the more usual binary coding of 1 and 0 is adopted, the storage rule must be slightly modified, and the number of patterns which can be stored in the memory is halved.

2.21 Conclusion

This chapter has introduced all the basic theory necessary to understand the three principal types of neural networks in use today. More advanced theoretical treatments may be found in Bishop (1995), Ripley (1996) and Hassoun (1995). A rapid search of the relevant scientific literature would reveal that the multi-layer perceptron is by far the most popular of the three network types. A deeper analysis of many of these papers would also reveal the many pitfalls associated with training and using MLPs. It is the aim of this book to enable its readers to avoid all of the possible pitfalls and to become proficient in neural computing, whether they are users of software packages or are developing their own code. Although it is not essential that all of the mathematical derivations presented in this chapter should be understood in their entirety, the mathematical treatment provides the theoretical justification for many of the practical points which are made later in the book.

3
MANAGING A NEURAL COMPUTING PROJECT

3.1 Introduction

IT project management is a highly developed discipline in its own right, and most of the practices of good IT project management apply to neural computing projects. This chapter introduces the features of the development life cycle which are unique to neural computing application development, and describes the implications of these features for project management. Consequently, the chapter supplements normal IT project management practice.

The chapter discusses principally the following issues:

- the key differences underlying the development of a neural computing application;
- the life cycle of the development project;
- project planning, monitoring and control;
- configuration management and documentation;
- the deliverable system.

3.2 Neural computing projects are different

Neural computing projects differ from many conventional software development projects for a number of reasons:

1. Projects are data driven. Therefore, there is a need to collect and analyse data as part of the design process and to train the neural network. This task is often time-consuming and the effort, resources and time required are frequently underestimated.

2. It is not usually possible to specify the solution fully at the design stage. Therefore, it is necessary to build prototypes and experiment with them in order to resolve design issues. This iterative development process can be difficult to control.

3. Performance, rather than speed of processing, is the key issue. More attention must be paid to performance issues during the requirements analysis,

design and test phases. Furthermore, demonstrating that the performance meets the requirements can be particularly difficult.

These issues will affect the following areas of management:

- **project planning**: plans should be made for the tasks of data collection, prototyping and neural network training, performance and design reviews, and system validation;
- **project management**: the iterative design optimisation process needs different techniques for planning, controlling and reviewing;
- **configuration management**: data management is an important part of the project; data and the results of experiments on this data must be integrated so that they can be linked to the appropriate design option;
- **documentation**: experimental results must be carefully recorded in a development log, and the documentation programme must be flexible enough to cope with the rapid evolution of the design that can occur in a typical neural computing project, but it is also essential that any given experiment can be repeated under exactly the same conditions.

3.3 The project life cycle

Figure 3.1 shows the typical project life cycle for a neural computing project from its original formulation to implementation and on-going maintenance. It is based on the standard IT project management model, adapted to include the elements unique to neural computing application development.

The project life cycle has three main phases:

1. application identification and feasibility;
2. development and validation of prototype;
3. conversion of prototype into deliverable system, delivery and maintenance.

The objectives of the first phase are the same as for any IT project, namely to identify applications and establish the feasibility and business case (if appropriate) for the proposed development. This phase will be considered in detail in the next chapter. It will be assumed, for the purposes of this chapter, that a suitable candidate application has been identified and that the feasibility study has been satisfactorily completed. The feasibility study should have been guided by a *requirements specification* document and the benchmark testing carried out towards the end of the study (see Chapter 4) will have given some idea of how difficult it will be to meet some of the requirements. The main requirement is always likely to be the desired *accuracy* (whether for a classification or for a regression problem) but the maximum number of inputs to the neural network may also be limited, given the time required to collect data and the fact that the number of training examples needed to train a neural network grows with the number of inputs[1].

Development and validation of prototype

The prototyping method is an iterative approach that leads to the refinement of the neural solution as shown in Figure 3.1. This method is a well-established technique for conventional IT projects, and is particularly appropriate for neural computing projects. Prototyping allows design decisions to be resolved through experimentation, and provides a number of other benefits:

- experiments can be carried out on sub-systems of the design;
- different hardware and software can be used for prototype and deliverable systems, allowing the most appropriate tools, languages and hardware to be used for each phase;
- the prototype can be validated before committing to the deliverable.

All of the experimentation required to resolve design issues will be part of the development and validation stage. This stage also includes the development of the neural network software and hence it is the principal focus of the rest of this book. Prototyping will affect the way the project is managed and the following sections in this chapter include advice on managing the problems of controlling the prototyping cycles.

The deliverable system, delivery and support

The final stage of the project, conversion of the prototype to the deliverable system, is concerned with converting the prototype into operational software and possibly hardware, and implementing any additional functions (for example, specific interfaces) that it requires. This stage is primarily concerned with software engineering and will differ little from the equivalent stages of a conventional IT project. Section 3.9 discusses the aspects of this phase that are different for a neural computing project.

3.4   Project planning

Project planning and control can be seen as a cyclic activity with three stages:

1. **plan**: plan to accommodate the project objectives, taking into account the risks and opportunities;
2. **act**: execute the plan while monitoring and controlling activities;
3. **review**: determine what has been achieved (and what has not), and use the conclusions as the input to the next planning activity.

---

[1] The relationship between the two is discussed in more detail in Chapter 6.

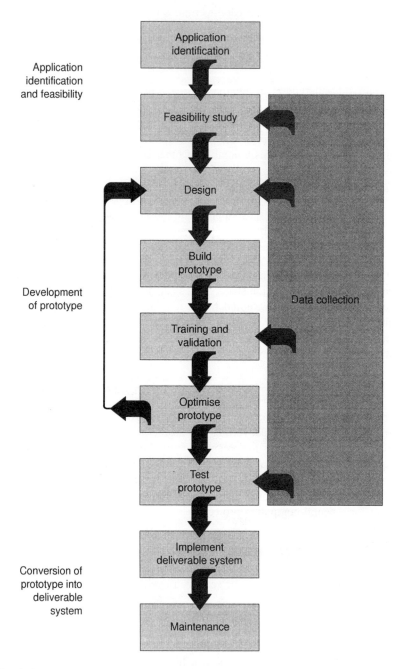

Fig. 3.1 *Typical neural computing project life cycle.*

This planning cycle is standard within conventional IT project management, and there are many methodologies for controlling it. Conventionally, it operates at two levels: at the overall project level, the work is split into a set of tasks with suitable review points, while at the lower level the individual tasks are subject to the same planning cycle.

In a prototyping project, a third, intermediate, level of planning cycle is added, and the management at this level is different from the management of more conventional projects. High-level planning is discussed below with reference to two areas particular to neural computing projects: prototyping and data collection.

High-level planning

The use of prototyping introduces a number of uncertainties into the planning process:

- the number of prototyping cycles required;
- the effort and time-scales for prototyping;
- the effort and time-scales for data collection.

These uncertainties will be greatest at the start of the project but, as the project progresses, many of these issues will become clearer and the plan can be refined. Consequently, reviewing and revising the high-level plan is particularly important and this should be done at regular intervals.

The first high-level plan should identify the main tasks and make an initial allocation of effort and time-scales. The effort and time-scales required for data collection will have to be estimated because the design and prototyping activities are dependent upon the availability of data. Indeed, the overall time-scales may be driven by the time taken to collect data, although the training of large networks can also have a significant influence on elapsed time.

Planning the prototyping cycle

It is vital to decide on (and document) the objectives for each prototyping cycle. Once these have been set, the effort and time-scales required can be estimated and detailed task descriptions can be drawn up.

In general, it is better to have a larger number of short prototyping cycles because, although they take more management effort, it is beneficial if the work is split into small segments. It is easier to set the objectives for each short cycle and thus keep the work going in the right direction.

Planning data collection

Planning and control of data collection is an important and often problematic part of managing a neural computing project. There are several major difficulties with data collection that can result in cost overruns and delays:

1. it can involve staff or organisations outside the direct control of the project manager;
2. it may involve complex and unfamiliar data acquisition equipment;
3. data collection may have to be interleaved with normal business activities.

Because the data collection activities often determine the time-scales for the whole project, they require realistic estimates of the time that it will take for the data to be collected. The following tasks need to be scheduled:

1. the main data collection exercise;
2. data conversion, if required;
3. data quality checking;

Other points to consider are:

- if special equipment or plant is needed, its availability should be scheduled;
- a document which specifies the data to be collected and procedures to be followed should be prepared. This is particularly important if data collection is to be performed by someone outside the project;
- the need to schedule one or more dry runs to check the procedures and ensure that any data conversion programs are correct.

Data quality checking is a very important topic. Incorrect labelling of data caused by transcription errors or faulty sensor readings can have very serious repercussions. During training, the neural network models will attempt to fit the erroneous data and this can lead to the generation of very poor models.

3.5 Project monitoring and control

Monitoring and control activities for neural computing projects are the same as with conventional projects: only the prototyping stage is different. This stage needs more detailed monitoring to determine when to terminate each iteration of prototyping. There are two situations in which it will be necessary to conclude an individual prototyping cycle earlier than planned:

1. when the goals for the prototyping cycle have been achieved early;
2. when the current work is unlikely to give satisfactory results.

If planning has been reasonably conservative, then there is a good chance that the goals will be achieved early, in which case the cycle should be stopped and the project moved on to the next cycle. On the other hand, there will also be instances where goals are not being achieved within budget, and a decision will have to be made as to whether to extend the work or terminate it.

3.6 Reviewing

Reviewing progress is a key part of an IT project management method, and neural computing projects are no different. However, there are three types of review that are particular to neural computing projects:

- data reviews;
- reviews at the end of each prototyping cycle;
- overall review at the end of the prototype development phase.

Data review

This should be carried out when all the data has been collected. The aim is to gain an understanding of the data and to determine whether it is sufficient for the requirements of the project. Decisions concerning the way in which the data should be partitioned into training, validation and test sets for a multi-layer perceptron or training and test sets for a radial basis function network also need to be made (see Chapter 2).

Prototype cycle performance review

At the end of each prototyping cycle, the following issues should be reviewed by the design and management teams:

- what has been learnt in terms of resolving design decisions?
- has adequate performance been achieved?
- is development complete?
- if not, which changes need to be implemented?

The requirements specification mentioned at the beginning of Section 3.3 should be used to assess progress towards the objectives set out in this document. The results of this assessment should form the basis for planning the next cycle of prototyping. It may be that the requirements specification will have to be modified in the light of the experience gained during the early prototyping cycles, although this is obviously a decision which could only be taken after consultation with every member of the project team, and only in exceptional circumstances.

Review at end of prototype development

It is vital to review the situation after the prototype has been developed and validated and before proceeding to the implementation of the deliverable system. The review should concentrate on determining the optimal technical solution (which may be based on a single prototype, or combine the best features of several experimental designs). In particular, it will be necessary to decide:

- whether to make marginal improvements to the prototype in order to complete the project;
- whether and how to implement the deliverable system.

The background relevant to these decisions is discussed at the end of this chapter in Section 3.9.

3.7 Configuration management

It is essential to manage the configuration of software and documents produced by the project, just as on a conventional computing project. In addition, with neural computing development work, there is a need to manage the configuration of data, experimental conditions and results. The prototyping phase will generate a large number of experimental results that will be used to determine the final system. The aim of the configuration management system must be to ensure that these results are recorded. Descriptions should include details of the exact conditions under which experiments are performed *so that they can be repeated* or the information used to make decisions on the design of the final system (the deliverable system).

Configuration management of data

The data collection exercise will produce a large quantity of data which will have been collected under different conditions at different times and possibly from different places. Managing this information collection process is vital, and procedures should be established to record (on paper or in a database) details of all the data files. Management information typically includes:

- filename;
- title;
- details of collection (time, date, equipment, etc.);
- collateral information (parameters not on data file);
- date created;
- version number;
- location (disk);
- details of any modifications (date, author, description, etc.).

Experimental conditions

Details of all experiments should be recorded in case they need to be repeated. Essential information includes:

- the version of the software used for the neural network, pre-processing and post-processing;

- the neural network architecture, topology, etc.;
- any parameters used in the pre-processing and post-processing;
- the data files used for training, validation and testing;
- details of the training (number of cycles, stopping criterion, etc.);
- the neural network weights (see below).

With most types of training algorithms, the initial weights are random values within a given range (see case studies in Chapter 8). Different sets of initial weights lead to different minima of the error function (see Chapter 2) and the files which record details of experimental conditions should include both the initial values of the network weights and those resulting from the training of the network with these initial values.

Experimental results

Experimental results should be recorded in engineering log books, and information logged should include data files, plots, dates, file names, versions, etc.

3.8   Documentation

With the exception of the design documentation and the performance summary, documentation for neural computing projects follows documentation schemes used for conventional software development. There are a number of differences in the way that neural computing project designs are documented, and these are discussed below. In general, the documentation should include:

- terms of reference/management plan;
- requirements specification;
- acceptance test specification;
- work plans and task descriptions;
- design documentation;
- program specifications;
- engineers' log books;
- test plans and results;
- user guide.

Design documentation

Documentation is a vital part of the design process: it is the means both of recording the design process and of specifying the final design (for implementation of the deliverable system). Different design documentation standards may be appropriate during different phases of the project:

- during the early design work and optimisation phases, a very flexible approach to documentation will be required since it is likely that the design will be changing more rapidly than would be the case in a conventional IT project;
- the design documentation scheme should support the designers' efforts to manage the evolving design. It should record the reasons for decisions taken, for example the reasons(s) for discarding an input variable or for deciding to run an extra experiment to acquire more data;
- at the early stages of a project, engineers' log books are recommended, but documentation for the final design should employ standard techniques.

Many conventional design documentation techniques such as data flow diagrams and data dictionaries will not be appropriate for neural computing techniques as they record the wrong kind of information. The design documentation must record information relevant to neural computing developments, such as the details of pre-processing algorithms, the neural network architecture and details of the training algorithm, including learning rate parameters and stopping criteria.

Performance summary

The performance summary is a document that provides the client or user with a summary of the performance of all the algorithms evaluated during the development phase. As well as providing a summary, it also constitutes an important factor in the final decisions about which algorithm should be implemented in the deliverable system. It should contain a brief description of the algorithms tested, the range of parameters used with them, and should summarise the performance statistics obtained during testing.

3.9 The deliverable system

Once the design and optimisation activities have been completed, there will exist a trained prototype which, along with the other elements of the deliverable system, must be implemented in its operating environment.

The scope of this implementation may vary from marginal improvements to the development version to a full re-implementation on a different hardware platform, possibly using special-purpose hardware. Full redesign and re-implementation may be required for a number of reasons:

- the deliverable system environment is different from the development environment;
- the deliverable system has special performance requirements, for example, real-time operation;

- the deliverable system has special interfacing requirements, for example, an interface to a plant or a special man-machine interface;
- the deliverable system has particular requirements for reliability.

The implementation should be treated as a separate project phase, and it will be very similar to the implementation phase of a conventional software project. Some design activities may be required, but these will be limited to refining the prototype system to run on implementation hardware and, possibly, designing any new functions such as special interfaces. This activity should be subject to conventional software engineering principles.

Although many aspects of implementation will be similar to a conventional IT project, acceptance testing and subsequent maintenance of the deliverable system deserve particular attention.

Acceptance testing

When the deliverable system has been implemented, the overall system will have to demonstrate the required functionality and performance. Although many of the techniques are the same, this is quite distinct from the performance validation procedures which are carried out on the prototype. In general, there is little in acceptance testing that is specific to neural computing except for the performance demonstration. As with any software testing, performance criteria should be agreed with the user and developed into a test plan. When preparing the test plan, the following should be considered:

- the performance metrics to be used. The primary performance metric, a measure of the system's performance on test data, is usually expressed in terms of accuracy, percentage correct classification, error rate or false alarm rate. This issue is discussed in more detail in Chapter 7 on the design of the prototype system;
- guaranteed and desirable performance levels;
- statistical tests and users' confidence in the results. This issue is the main determinant of the number of acceptance test cases that have to be run;
- the acceptance test cases to be used. These should be designed both to demonstrate the performance under normal operating conditions and to explore the range of input values for which the system gives acceptable results;
- whether adequate test data is available, particularly at the extremes of the system's operating range.

It should be borne in mind, however, that it is generally easier to compile detailed records of the performance of the trained neural network on the development platform, given its greater flexibility and power.

User handover and software maintenance

The user handover and training procedures are largely similar to those for conventional software projects. However, users should be made aware of the application's limitations, in particular that it may become unreliable if the input data is significantly outside the range of the training data (see the section at the end of Chapter 7 on 'extrapolation rather than interpolation').

Maintaining a neural computing application is also similar to maintaining conventional software. It will involve bug fixing and system enhancement. However, a key difference for neural computing systems is the need to maintain the performance of the system as well as its function. During development, the neural network was trained on data collected from the operating environment, probably over a limited period of time. For some applications, the operating environment will change over time, possibly leading to a reduction of performance. If this possibility is recognised before handover, provision can be made for occasional re-training of the deliverable system. This option should only be exercised in extreme cases, however, and only in close consultation with the designers of the prototype and deliverable systems.

4
IDENTIFYING APPLICATIONS AND ASSESSING THEIR FEASIBILITY

4.1   Introduction

Neural computing is only suited to certain types of problem. Within an appropriate problem domain, however, the correct application of neural computing techniques will bring significant advantages. This begs the question: when should one use a neural computing solution?

It is important to reiterate the fact that information about the problem domain is captured in a radically different way in neural computing. With traditional computing, the information used to solve the problem is transparent to the user of the software; it is encoded *explicitly* in the program written to solve the problem, for example in a series of IF-THEN-ELSE statements. With neural computing, the information is encoded *implicitly* in the network weights; as we have already seen, the relationship between the input variables and the target data is *learnt* during the training of the network when the weights are gradually modified as the set of training examples is repeatedly presented to the network (see Chapter 2). Once the network has been trained, it is not possible to infer directly from the network weights *how* the network is solving the problem. In most applications, this is not necessarily a disadvantage. However, it is a legal requirement for some information processing systems that they should be capable of providing an explanation for any decision made as a result of their use. It is therefore not surprising that the extraction of rules from trained networks is currently an active research area (see, for example, Corbett-Clark and Tarassenko, 1997, and Setiono, 1997).

In this chapter, we review the issues which should be considered when deciding whether a given problem lends itself to a neural network solution. This is followed by a brief review of examples of successful applications of neural computing. We then investigate how the feasibility of candidate applications may be assessed starting from the technical point of view and finishing with consideration of a business case for industrial applications. (It is possible, if not probable, that the business case may have to be put together *before* any feasibility study takes place.) The importance of data collection and data understanding is emphasised throughout.

4.2 Identifying neural computing applications

There are three main criteria which need to be applied when deciding whether a given problem lends itself to a neural computing approach:

1. The solution to the problem cannot be explicitly described by an algorithm, a set of equations (representing a physical model, for example), or a set of rules.
2. There is some evidence that an input–output mapping exists between a set of input variables x and corresponding output data y, such that $y = f(x)$. The form of f, however, is not known.
3. There should be a large amount of data available, i.e. many different examples with which to train the network.

Let us now examine each one of these in some detail:

Criterion 1. *The problem cannot be explicitly described by a set of equations or a set of rules.*

Making the decision between a conventional and a neural computing solution on the basis of the above criterion is not always entirely clear cut. There are problems for which both conventional *and* neural computing may be able to provide appropriate solutions. The choice then depends on the resources available and the ultimate goals of the project. Take, by way of illustration, the problem of weather prediction. Accurate medium- to long-term forecasting requires very complex models backed up by regular observations of atmospheric conditions over sea and land. On the other hand, there is no reason why a neural network could not be trained to predict tomorrow's weather *locally* based on today's weather and local measurements of temperature, pressure and humidity. The problem might be configured as a three-class problem, the three network outputs being the probabilities of tomorrow being sunny, cloudy or rainy. The inputs to the network would be today's weather (sunny, cloudy or rainy, as binary variables) and the measurements of today's temperature, pressure and humidity (as continuous variables). The record of this data for a complete year should be sufficient to provide a data set for training a 6-input, 3-output network to predict the next day's local weather. Unless weather conditions occurred which were significantly different from those found in the training data set, the trained network would be expected to perform with reasonable accuracy on new data.

Criterion 2. *There is some evidence that an input–output mapping exists between a set of input variables x and corresponding output data y such that $y = f(x)$.*

In the weather prediction example, one is using knowledge that there is some correlation between today's and tomorrow's weather and the fact that the weather depends, to some extent, on temperature, pressure and humidity. The fact that a database with a set of input and output variables can be assembled does *not* necessarily mean, however, that a mapping can be constructed between the input variables and the target data. There would be no point, for example, in attempting to train a weather prediction network with input variables such as the day of the week and the sunrise and sunset times.

It is generally true that successful neural network solutions rely on the use of *prior* knowledge about the problem domain. Often, this knowledge will be crucial in the selection of the most appropriate features to characterise the problem. In the case of supervised learning, neural networks establish high-order (non-linear) correlations between the input features x and the output data y in order to minimise the output error. No matter how good the learning algorithm is, however, this will not happen unless *relevant* features are used as the input to the network.

Criterion 3. *There should be large amounts of data available, i.e. many different examples with which to train the network.*

Neural networks require large quantities of data at every stage of development, both input data and target data for an application which requires supervised learning. If there are any doubts about the availability of data, then in all probability the project should not proceed: lack of suitable data is one of the main causes of problems during neural computing development projects. If such data has not yet been collected and compiled in a computer readable form, then it will be necessary to collect data as part of the project. There may, however, be considerable practical problems associated with this; special instrumentation and recording facilities may be required, and specific experiments may be needed to ensure that the data covers the necessary range of conditions. For example, if a neural network is to be incorporated in a monitoring or control capacity in an air-conditioning plant, data corresponding to all expected values of temperature and humidity (both in summer and winter) will have to be acquired.

4.3 Typical examples of neural computing applications

Candidate applications may be found in many problem domains. They might be found in a production process, within a business process such as forecasting, sales or marketing, or they could be part of the product itself. Table 4.1 indicates potential areas for the application of neural computing techniques.

There are now examples of the successful application of neural networks to most of the problem domains highlighted in Table 4.1. For example, in the condition monitoring field, neural networks have been trained to identify subtle changes in the vibration spectra of jet engines (Nairac *et al.*, 1997a and 1997b). There have been numerous papers published on the application of neural networks to financial forecasting, indeed several books (see, for example, Refenes,

	Fault diagnosis	Condition monitoring	Forecasting	Signal/Image analysis	Pattern detection in databases	Industrial inspection	Fraud detection	Process modelling and control
Part manufacturing	✓	✓				✓		
Process manufacturing		✓					✓	✓
Retailing			✓		✓		✓	
Finance and Insurance			✓		✓		✓	
Engineering	✓	✓		✓				✓
Production control	✓		✓					✓
Service			✓		✓			
Treasury function			✓				✓	
Sales and Marketing			✓		✓			

Table 4.1 *Typical business functions and neural computing application areas.*

1995 and Kingdon, 1997). Likewise, the fields of image and signal analysis have proved fertile ground for the application of neural network techniques. In *medical* image and signal analysis, there have been at least two neural network systems which have been developed all the way to commercial exploitation: PAPNET, a smart prompting system for the analysis of cervical smears (Boon and Kok, 1995) and QUESTAR (QUantification of EEG and Sleep Technologies Analysis and Review), a neural network analysis system (Pardey *et al.*, 1996b) capable of analysing the brain's electrical activity in patients suffering from severe sleep disorders. (One of the two case studies in Chapter 8 is based on data similar to that used to train the QUESTAR system.) Both PAPNET and QUESTAR have recently obtained Food & Drugs Administration (FDA) approval in the United States, an indication of neural computing's increasing maturity. There are also neural computing systems commercially available for Pattern Detection in Databases and Fraud Detection: Relationship Marketing™ for Database Mining from Recognition Systems and the Countermatch Signature™ Verification System from AEA Technology.

The above list is by no means exhaustive and is intended merely to indicate that there are now well-documented neural computing solutions across a wide spectrum of applications.

4.4 Preliminary assessment of candidate application

After a candidate application has been identified, the first step should be to verify that the three criteria of Section 4.2 can be met in full. If a candidate application does not possess all of the required attributes associated with these criteria, then neural computing is very unlikely to provide an appropriate solution.

The next step is to consider a number of practical issues:

1. Are adequate resources available? There is always a significant learning curve associated with a venture into a new technology.
2. Are there any objections that may be raised concerning the new technology? For example, safety-critical or business-critical applications require a higher level of validation. If this cannot be provided, the application may not go ahead. Alternatively, the neural network may be operated within an externally provided safety envelope. It should also be noted that the issue of validation and verification of neural networks is one which is receiving significant attention at the moment (Morgan and Austin, 1995; Lowe and Zapart, 1997).
3. Are there any practical problems associated with the collection of the data? As already mentioned in Section 4.2, the training of a neural network requires data to be collected over the entire range of operation. This may need special instrumentation and/or specific experiments to be designed.

The important topic of data collection will feature again in this chapter and later on in the text, but the need to consider it at an early stage cannot be over-emphasised.

Once an application has passed the preliminary assessment stage described above, a feasibility study should be undertaken. Once again, the unique features of neural computing will have an impact on how such a feasibility study should be carried out. It should certainly cover the following areas:

- the technical feasibility of developing the application;
- the availability and type of data as well as the cost of data collection;
- the preparation of the business case, if appropriate.

Each of these is now reviewed in turn.

4.5 Technical feasibility

It is assumed that, by the time this stage has been reached, the potential user of neural computing techniques has acquired a sufficient degree of familiarity with them (without necessarily having had any practical experience). A thorough literature search for references to related work should be carried out at this stage. As indicated earlier on in this chapter, neural computing now has a large applications literature and it is highly likely that there are papers on applications similar to the one under consideration. The quality of the papers in the neural network literature, however, is highly variable and some of the papers may contain the type of mistakes highlighted in the last few pages of Chapter 7 (Section 7.9).

Once the literature search has been carried out, an outline design should be prepared as early as possible in the feasibility study stage. This may only be a paper exercise, but it could extend to the collection of a sample of data and even to some prototyping work. It should include consideration of pre-processing (which features best characterise the problem?) and a preliminary assessment of the required neural network architecture. The issues of pre-processing and choice of features are also considered in more detail in Chapter 7.

Although the performance requirements cannot usually be defined precisely at this stage, an estimate of the level of performance required should be attempted. There are a number of factors which indicate whether appropriate performance may be difficult to achieve. For example:

- the main discriminating factors are not present in the available data. An example of this would be an attempt to develop a neural network to assess mortgage applications without having any knowledge of the applicants' salaries;
- the network is required to discriminate between many different classes;
- the network has a very large number of inputs (several hundreds, for example);
- the network is required to implement a very complex function;
- the network has to distinguish between very similar cases with a very high degree of accuracy;
- the training data does not represent the range of cases that the network will encounter. A neural network must be trained over all its eventual operating conditions.

4.6 Data availability and cost of collection

Training data is essential to the success of neural computing application development, and the availability and quality of training data should be confirmed at the feasibility study stage. The range of data available to train the neural network should be representative of the data that the network will have to process once trained. It should also include examples of extreme input conditions so that it will perform correctly at these extremes. If at all possible, a representative sample of the input data should be acquired in order to make a preliminary analysis of it. Data visualisation techniques (such as Kohonen's feature map) are very useful in this context and this point will be clearly brought out in the case studies of Chapter 8.

If the data is not immediately available, the feasibility of collecting it will have to be assessed; this can be a major exercise in its own right. In many situations, there will be both practical problems and cost implications associated with collecting data. For example, the training data for a fault diagnosis system should represent various fault conditions but simulating these on large items of equipment may be impractical for cost or safety reasons.

4.7 The business case

If the neural computing application is being developed in industry, then it is likely that a business case will have to be put together in order to justify the proposed project to senior management. This will be similar to that prepared for any new project, but there are a number of factors relating to the introduction of a new technology, some relating to neural computing, that fall outside the usual business case parameters. The three standard elements of the business case will be costs, benefits and risks.

Cost

The majority of the costs will be the same as for any new application development. However, there are certain costs that are specific to a neural computing application, and there may be costs associated with acquiring the technology.

As with any software cost estimation, a work breakdown based on the outline design forms the basis for an estimate of the effort required, and hence the cost. Many of the elements will be the same as for conventional software development, and conventional estimating techniques can be used for these. Two further elements are specific to neural computing:

- the collection, preparation and analysis of the training data;
- the design, training and testing of the neural network (i.e. the prototyping cycle).

The importance of the first of these has already been emphasised in this chapter. The cost implications of data collection and analysis are as follows:

1. If the data has to be collected, the cost of any equipment that might be required for data collection needs to be included.
2. If the data is already available, it will be necessary to make an accurate estimate of the effort required to transfer the data onto the platform to be used for neural network development. This should include the costs of any re-formatting required for this platform.
3. If data is being collected from production plant or machinery, it may be necessary to include the costs of having that plant or machinery out of action. Similarly, the costs of having to acquire data that fully characterises the operation of the plant need to be borne in mind.

4. If the proposed neural network uses supervised learning, it is important to determine who is going to label the data, the time that this will require and how much it will therefore cost.

Benefits

The business case should obviously describe the benefits to be obtained from implementing a neural computing solution. The process of assessing potential benefits will be similar to that required when introducing any other new technology. In general, the technical attributes of the neural computing solution should bring into business benefits such as:

- automation of manual processes may result in reduced staff costs;
- improved forecasting performance may result in improved stock control which, in turn, may result in lower cost of maintaining stock;
- earlier detection of faults may result in reduced plant downtime which, in turn, may result in reduced maintenance costs and higher productivity;
- improved plant monitoring may result in better performance which, in turn, may result in lower production costs;
- improved recognition of faulty components may result in better product quality which, in turn, may result in more satisfied customers and reduced re-work costs;
- more effective analysis of a customer database may result in better targeting of marketing resources and, therefore, a higher return from a marketing investment.

Risks

Risk assessment is an essential component of any new undertaking, and the majority of risks will be similar to those for the introduction of any new or leading edge technology, namely:

- shortfall of performance;
- poor technical knowledge resulting in poor choice of application or poor design;
- user resistance;
- the difficulty of meeting expectations if the potential benefits are oversold.

Two areas in neural computing projects carry extra risks:

- there are often significant risks of cost or time overruns associated with data collection, particularly if this involves doing experiments on large or costly equipment;
- it is often difficult to predict the performance that can be achieved, and this can lead to performance shortfalls or to increased development times.

The second of these can be alleviated if the potential performance is estimated with a simple (non-neural) technique. For example, in a classification problem, the nearest-neighbour technique (Bishop, 1995) gives an idea of the classification rate which should at the very least be achieved by the neural network. A nearest-neighbour classifier is extremely simple to implement. Input patterns are assigned the class of the pattern which is nearest to them (in Euclidean distance) in input space. The implementation of a nearest-neighbour classifier as soon as sufficient data has been acquired is highly recommended (see Chapter 8).

4.8 Conclusion

In this chapter, we have proposed three criteria for identifying potential applications of neural computing. Neural networks are especially useful for problems whose solutions cannot be described by a set of equations or a set of rules. There should be some evidence, however, that a relationship is likely to exist between the input variables and the answers sought at the output of the network. Good-quality training data is essential and this is a requirement which has featured prominently throughout this chapter. If at all possible, a representative sample of the input data should be acquired early on during the feasibility study. In some cases, it will be very helpful to visualise the distribution of the data using 2-D visualisation techniques such as Kohonen's feature map.

It is also important that the feasibility study should establish some kind of benchmark performance using at least one non-neural technique. There are many instances of papers in the literature which oversell neural networks because the authors have not evaluated the neural computing solution against a more traditional pattern recognition technique. If the problem is one of prediction, then a *linear* predictive model should be applied to the data first (Weigend and Gershenfeld, 1993; Masters, 1995) in order to determine a minimum level of performance. Similarly, for classification problems, the traditional statistical methods of quadratic and linear discriminants (James, 1985; Bishop, 1995) could be applied to the data as an initial attempt to classify it. These methods assume a multivariate normal (Gaussian) distribution for the data. Alternatively, a linear classifier trained to minimise the Mean Squared Error (MSE) at the output and nearest-neighbour classification techniques can both be implemented very quickly on a representative sample of data and they will also provide an estimate of the minimum level of performance required for the neural computing solution. This will be the strategy adopted for the case studies of Chapter 8.

5
NEURAL COMPUTING
HARDWARE AND SOFTWARE

5.1   Introduction

In the influential review article already mentioned at the beginning of Chapter 1, Lippmann (1987) wrote: '*The greatest potential of neural nets remains in the high-speed processing that could be provided through massively parallel VLSI implementations.*' The notion that massive parallelism is a key advantage of neural networks is no longer prevalent today, although massively parallel implementations based on analogue VLSI or optical technology continue to be active research topics. Nowadays, most neural network applications are developed, tested and run on PCs or standard workstations.

The selection of the platform for a neural network system will be based primarily on that system's computational requirements. These are examined in the section that follows before the issue of software tools is dealt with briefly. The chapter ends with consideration of special-purpose hardware.

5.2   Computational requirements

Pre-processing

Before we can consider the computational requirements in detail, brief mention must be made of pre-processing. It is rare that raw data is presented to the input of a neural network; in most applications, some form of pre-processing is applied in order to extract the information of most relevance. The range of pre-processing functions includes Fourier transforms and filtering of signals or images. In the case study (see Chapter 8) which focuses on medical signal analysis, the information of interest in the signal under consideration, the electroencephalogram, is in the frequency domain and hence a pre-processor is used to convert the signal on a second-by-second basis into a set of coefficients which encode the dominant frequencies in the spectrum. This illustrates the point that the pre-processing may occasionally make greater computational demands than the implementation of the trained neural network.

Training versus executing the network

There are two separate requirements when considering the computational power required for a particular neural network application:

1. the computational requirements for *executing* or *running* a trained neural network;
2. the computational requirements for *training* the neural network.

The first of these has usually been measured in the number of connections processed each second. A connection is a path from one neuron to another, including the associated weight, and processing a connection normally involves a multiply-and-accumulate operation followed by a sigmoid function (MLP) or an Euclidean distance computation followed by exponentiation (RBF network). This measure is often referred to as 'connections-per-second' (CPS) or, more often, as 'millions of connections-per-second' (MCPS). However, the published figures often fail to account for various processing overheads and the connections-per-second measure is highly dependent upon the neural network architecture. Thus the MCPS measure is of little value unless the quoted figure is based on a network architecture similar to the one under consideration. For networks with small numbers of connections, the dominant factor is *not* the number of connections processed but the time it takes to compute the sigmoid activation function for a neuron in an MLP or the exponentiation for a hidden unit in an RBF network.

Finally, quoted speeds often assume that the entire test set can be held in memory, rather than having to be accessed from slower devices such as a hard disk. The likely size of the data set compared to the available memory can therefore have a significant effect on the value of MCPS which can be achieved.

For the *training* of the network, the index of interest is the number of connection *updates* per second, usually expressed in 'millions of connection updates per second' (MCUPS). This is a fairly easy figure to establish for the training of an MLP as it simply requires a knowledge of how long it takes to compute the weight update equations for the error back-propagation algorithm (see Chapter 2 and Appendix A) for that platform. For an RBF network, it is less obvious how an MCUPS index can be calculated, given the two-phase nature of the training algorithm and the fact that the free parameters of the first layer are centre positions and widths, rather than weights *per se*.

To summarise, there are two questions to be answered when considering the computational requirements of a neural network application:

- Which *index* should be used for performance evaluation? (MCPS or MCUPS)?
- Which *benchmark problem* should be chosen for performance evaluation?

The answer to the first question depends on whether the application is likely to require significant development time. If large numbers of networks have to be trained before the optimal network is found (for example, whilst trying to evaluate the discriminatory power of large numbers of features or carrying out exhaustive searches on the optimal number of hidden units), then the MCUPS index is the more important as it will have a strong influence on the development time. If, on the other hand, the problem is already well defined because of prior knowledge, the development may be considerably shorter and the user will be more interested in the execution time for the trained network. It should be remembered, however, that it can be difficult to predict the final form of a particular solution because neural computing applications are usually developed iteratively.

The second question itself raises further questions. Performance on a benchmark problem depends on the network architecture, the learning algorithm and the precision (number of bits) required during the training or execution of the network. Different problems are more or less suited to a particular architecture and/or learning algorithm and it is therefore preferable to consider performance on a number of benchmark problems rather than a single test problem. To get away from MCPS or MCUPS, it may be preferable to use the following indices of performance:

1. the time taken to classify one pattern, when considering the *running* of a trained neural network classifier;
2. the time taken to complete an epoch of learning[1], when assessing the *training* of an MLP; for an RBF network, the very fast nature of two-phase training (see Section 2.17) means that the only meaningful criterion would be the total training time under tightly-specified conditions: K-means for optimisation of the centre positions followed by matrix inversion or a fixed number of iterations of the LMS algorithm.

5.3 Platforms for software solutions

Broadly speaking, there are two neural network development software options:

1. commercial development packages or tools;
2. writing your own software.

Neural network development packages are now widely available and run on conventional computers ranging from PCs through to mainframes. These packages provide the software for training a network and for executing it once training is complete. Many packages interface with standard spreadsheets, from which they obtain their input data. This provides a flexible environment for designing, training and testing the neural network. The outputs will usually be displayed on the screen and written to a file.

---

[1]Updating all of the weights for each pattern presentation and presenting all of the patterns in the training set once.

The market for neural computing development products is still evolving. Currently, most packages require at least a working knowledge of different neural network architectures and of the training algorithms, and of the suitability of each for a particular application.

Typically, the preferred platform is either a PC or a standard workstation. Either can be combined with a special hardware accelerator or parallel processor cards to give increased computational power and resources, if required. It is important to ensure that the selected platform could be expanded to deal with extra demands on memory, disk capacity or processor power. In particular, the option of using memory caching or memory disks to access large amounts of data should be considered. The availability of a processing accelerator option (see below) may also affect the choice of platform.

Platforms for neural network development

The criteria for selection of the development platform will be price, availability, the ability to run the chosen software, and the computing power required for training.

When choosing the hardware platform, you should ensure that:

- it has sufficient processing power to cope with the computations required during neural network training;
- it has the disk capacity to hold the expected volumes of data, including both the training data and the network parameters (weights and/or centre positions and widths);
- any special computing equipment or interface hardware that may be required during the data collection phase is considered in the planning phase.

Commercial packages

It is unlikely that a complete application can be developed using a commercial package alone. Generally, multiple development tools, or a mixture of tools and bespoke code, will be required, and it is vital to check that the tools have adequate facilities for importing and exporting data. It is important to check also whether the packages support common data interfaces and whether the neural network software can be linked directly to spreadsheet or database packages. If the development of an application using a bought-in software package is successful, then its commercial exploitation will not proceed until the issue of the licensing of the software has been considered.

A recent review of well-known packages may be found in James (1997). Most neural computing development packages allow the neural network structure to be edited (for example, the number of layers and units within them). However, if the number of input or output units is changed, the data file input and output variables will no longer match the network, and the neural software package should allow the data file to be modified to overcome this problem.

Commercial packages fall into three main categories:

1. entry level packages, aimed at the interested novice;
2. project development packages, aimed at industrial and commercial users;
3. academic packages, aimed at researchers.

Entry level packages

Entry level packages provide facilities for experimenting with neural networks. In general, they are inexpensive products written for PCs. The facilities tend to be limited with MLPs often the only architecture which is supported. Most are well documented and have reasonable simulation facilities: they can deliver simple complete applications and some packages can be upgraded to a more advanced version. These provide a seamless path from entry level functionality to advanced facilities.

Project development packages

There are also neural computing development systems available which combine special hardware (usually as a co-processor board) with simulation software that exploits the hardware's capabilities. They are designed for the development and delivery of complete neural computing applications, and may offer several neural network architectures and training methods.

Academic packages

Academic or research neural network simulators provide a wide range of neural network architectures and training methods, as well as access to the mathematics that underlie neural computing. Some also offer pre-processing and post-processing functions for application development. These packages are especially useful for algorithm development as opposed to application work.

Public domain software

Public domain software (i.e. software that is distributed for free use) is available for neural network processing. The software ranges from complete packages to source code for implementing various functions and routines. Unfortunately, most public domain software has not been rigorously tested and is more likely to contain bugs than commercially developed code. Therefore, public domain software can be useful in providing a first taste of neural computing, but caution should be exercised before using it for a commercial development project.

Writing your own software

Writing prototype code from scratch is not necessary but will provide a deeper understanding of the algorithms. In general, this also provides greater flexibility during development. If the user has no prior experience, then the software that he or she writes can initially be checked against the results obtained with a validated commercial package.

5.4 Special-purpose hardware

While many neural computing applications can be developed on a standard PC or workstation, some neural network systems have very high computational power requirements, either for the neural network itself, for the pre-processing or for both. Two approaches are appropriate:

- accelerator systems for fast calculations;
- special-purpose hardware designed for neural computing, often with multiple processors.

High-speed accelerator systems are available for both standard PCs and for workstations. They come in many forms: some are complete stand-alone systems which link to the host platform, while others are cards which plug into the host platform.

In order to train large networks in reasonable time, dedicated hardware may be required and a number of special-purpose digital VLSI systems have been designed in the last few years. Manufacturers of such products have tended to describe them as *neurocomputers*, the best known examples of these being the CNAPS^{TM} machine (from Adaptive Solutions Inc. in the US) and the SYNAPSE-1^{TM} (from Siemens in Germany).

The Connected Network of Adaptive Processors (CNAPS) is a Single Instruction Multiple Data (SIMD) array of digital signal processor-like computing elements described as 'Processor Nodes' (PNs). The array is laid out in one dimension and operates synchronously. Data representation is digital *fixed point*. The CNAPS machine is capable of operating in different precision modes, the preferred option being 8-bit data and 16-bit weights. Adaptive Solutions claim that a single CNAPS chip can be used for the NETtalk benchmark problem (see Section 7.4 in Chapter 7 for a description of this problem), with the complete training cycle – using an unspecified size of database – taking only 7 seconds as compared to 4 hours with a Sun Sparc1 workstation, i.e. a speed-up factor of 2 000. (Note that the comparison is with a Sparc1 workstation. A more recent workstation would probably be 50 to 100 times faster.)

Siemens' Neurocomputer, SYNAPSE-1, has eight 'neural signal processors', each one of these being a 610 000-transistor full-custom VLSI chip with 32 Mb of local memory. The SYNAPSE-1 Neurocomputer also includes a data unit and a control unit, both of which are based on the MC68040 CPU (Motorola). The control unit also handles communication with a host computer which is part of the neurocomputer. Siemens claim (Ramacher *et al.*, 1993) that the SYNAPSE-1 is '8 000 times faster than a Sun Sparc2 workstation'. Again, there is little value in this claim, as there is no indication whether it is for training or running a network, and neither the benchmark problem nor the neural network architecture are specified in support of the claim.

Evaluation criteria for special-purpose hardware

The SYNAPSE-1 project leader listed the following set of requirements for a neurocomputer:

- it must have a computing power that is at least three orders of magnitude greater than existing workstations;
- it must support small, medium and large-scale neural networks to handle the full range of neural network applications;
- it must have a general-purpose architecture that can support all known neural networks;
- it must have a user interface that makes it accessible to a large range of researchers, developers and customers.

These criteria are very laudable but do not address the issues raised in Section 5.2: which index is to be used to evaluate the neurocomputer's computational power (MCPS, MCUPS or other) and which benchmark problems are considered to be appropriate for testing across a significant range of architectures and learning algorithms? One further question is whether the neurocomputer is capable of supporting 'virtual networks'; in other words, how would it cope with networks larger than the physical size of the VLSI multiplier array?

The advantages of a neurocomputer (or any special-purpose hardware) always have to be assessed against the flexibility provided by a general-purpose workstation with good floating-point capabilities. In addition, Digital Signal Processing (DSP) microprocessors, whilst retaining the flexibility of general-purpose processors, are also optimised for multiply-accumulate operations (i.e. the weighted summations found in every layer of an MLP). In a DSP microprocessor, the digital multiplier/accumulator is integrated into the data path; thus, the arithmetic is not performed on a co-processor separated from the main data path but instead it is an integral part of the execution of every instruction. As a result, one multiply-and-accumulate operation can be performed with *every instruction cycle* (a full 32-bit floating point multiply and add in 40 ns, i.e. 25 MFLOPS[2], is now standard). The limitation, of course, is the serial mode of operation of these devices, but for small to medium network sizes—which still represent the vast majority of applications—they are likely to be very competitive with the neurocomputers described above.

---

[2]Note that there can be ambiguity in the calculation of MFLOPS (Mega FLoating-point Operations Per Second): since most hardware multipliers perform a multiply-and-add operation in one cycle, the latter is normally treated as *one* FLOP, as in the above calculation; if the multiply *and* the add are counted as two separate operations, then the multiply-and-add operation is equivalent to 2 FLOPS instead.

It should also be remembered that the length of the design cycle means that special-purpose neurocomputers are often not very competitive by the time they become available. (As computer power doubles every year, today's neurocomputer can be guaranteed to be superseded sooner or later by a general-purpose computer.) Except for very large networks, the best *neuro*computer may simply be a general-purpose computer with good floating-point arithmetic capabilities.

5.5 Deliverable system

Often, the code size and processing requirement overheads of development tools preclude their use in the deliverable system (which is taken to be here the *trained* neural network plus memory and input/output ports). However, some tools can produce code that can be used by the deliverable system; others can, in addition, be used to implement a user interface for the neural network. These are facilities more likely to be found in the more expensive tools, but they can result in significant saving to the overall project cost. The cost of a development tool is likely to be small compared with the overall cost of a project and, even if its cost is high, it is generally wise to choose a tool that will reduce the project development effort.

Most often, neural computing applications are developed in software running on a PC or standard workstation. The final, deliverable system may also be implemented to run on a PC or workstation, with or without the support of accelerator cards. Less often, the deliverable system may be implemented in special-purpose hardware.

Different hardware platforms can be used for development and deliverable systems, allowing the most appropriate combination of software and hardware for each phase. Conversely, the hardware platform(s) chosen for the development and delivery phases will impose constraints on the choice of neural network software, special hardware (for example, accelerators) and the development tools available to solve the problem.

6
COLLECTING AND PREPARING DATA

6.1 Introduction

It is obvious from the life cycle model in Figure 3.1 that data collection is a major part of a neural computing project. Often, it runs in parallel with the other project activities because data is required in different quantities at different stages. Planning the data collection so that sufficient data is available at the right points in the project is vital to the success of the project.

Neural networks are data-driven models and the quality of the model is therefore highly dependent on the quality of the data used to train it. Neural networks are particularly good at combining different types of data from different sources, a process known as *data fusion*. For example, the state of a motor (prediction of a single output variable) could be determined by a network trained on measurements of sound, temperature, vibrations and flow rate of the lubricant.

A word of warning needs to be introduced at the outset, however: data of insufficient quality or in insufficient quantity will prevent the development of the neural computing application from being successful. Data collection, preparation and understanding are therefore critical in neural computing projects.

6.2 Glossary

A glossary of terms related to data in the context of neural computing is included here for reference. Most of the terms have already been introduced in previous chapters but a few of them are given a more formal definition in this glossary.

- **input data**: data which is applied to the input of the neural network during training or operation;
- **input vector**: a set of input data for a particular example. (A vector here is taken to be a vector of numbers, i.e. $x = (x_1, x_2, \ldots, x_n)$, where x_n is the nth measurement or feature value);
- **labelling**: the process of associating input vectors with corresponding target vectors for supervised learning;

- **output data**: the neural network's output values during training or operation;
- **output vector**: a set of output data for a particular example;
- **data partitioning**: the process of dividing the available data into training, validation (if needed) and test sets;
- **target data**: data which acts as a target during training for the values of the output data. The output data of a neural network is compared with target data (the 'desired' set of values) during training and during performance testing;
- **target vector**: a set of target data for a particular example;
- **test set**: a set of data, which the neural network has not previously seen, and which is used to test performance. The performance test measures how well the neural network has learned to generalise. In the neural computing literature, the test set is sometimes also referred to as the 'generalisation set';
- **training set**: a set of data which is used for training a neural network, i.e. for adapting the weights of the network until the stopping criterion is met;
- **validation set**: a set of data used to test the performance of the network during training *but not used for modifying the weights of the network* (see Section 2.9 on 'Training a Multi-layer Perceptron');
- **stopping criterion**: if a validation set is being used during supervised learning, the stopping criterion will be the point at which the minimum error on the validation set is reached. Alternatively, the stopping criterion can simply be a fixed number of iterations (passes through the training set).

6.3 Data requirements

The nature of the data required for a neural computing application is highly dependent on the application. In general, both relevant and possibly relevant data should be considered as inputs to the neural network. It is not necessary to know the nature of the relationship between the input data x and the target output y, only that there is a strong possibility that there is a relationship. The neural network will determine an approximation to the function f (where $y = f(x)$) during the training process.

If the application is one of prediction or classification, learning will be supervised and target data as well as input data will have to be collected. For prediction problems, the target data will consist of the desired value associated with each input vector; for classification problems, it will be the correct class for that input vector. Expert assistance may be needed for the task of labelling the data.

How much data?

It is important to make a reasonable estimate of how much data is required to train the neural network properly. If too little data is collected, the full range of the relationship that the neural network should be learning may not be covered. We need to have sufficient data points for the form of the function f to be specified accurately enough throughout the whole of input space. Bishop (1995) introduces a useful analogy in the first chapter of his book *Neural Networks for Pattern Recognition*. To a first approximation, neural networks can be likened to polynomial curve fitting. In this context, generalisation can be seen as *interpolation* between the training examples. As with any other curve-fitting technique, neural networks cannot extrapolate reliably; if there is no training data in a region of input space from which some of the test data is drawn, then there cannot be any valid generalisation for those test patterns. The network, of course, will always give an answer but this answer will be no better than guesswork.

Thus a sufficient number of training examples is required to ensure that the neural network is trained to recognise and respond to the full range of conditions (including normal operation as well as fault conditions) that it will encounter when analysing test data. For similar reasons, in classification problems, it is best, if at all possible, to assemble a *balanced* database in which all the classes are equally well represented. We will return to this issue from a slightly different perspective in the next chapter.

Number of training examples

Information theory suggests that the number of training examples (i.e. the number of input vectors in the training set) should be of the same order as the number of free parameters in the network. The free parameters are the network weights which are adjusted when the training examples are presented at the input to the network. The number of weights, W, for an I-J-K multi-layer perceptron is given by:

$$W = (I + 1)J + (J + 1)K \tag{6.1}$$

where, as before, I is the number of inputs, J the number of hidden units and K the number of output units in the network. We have assumed, as in Chapter 2, that each of the hidden and output units has a bias weight associated with it. Thus the first estimate for the required number of training patterns, P is that it should at least be equal to W.

From a different starting point, Widrow and Lehr (1990) argue that the number of training patterns should be evaluated in terms of the *network capacity*, the ratio of the number of weights to the number of classes, i.e. W/K. The concept of network capacity arose in the early 1960s when the ability of single-layer networks to assign input vectors to one of two classes was investigated in depth, leading to a number of fundamental theorems. In their 1990 paper, Widrow and

Lehr attempt to extend this theory to multi-layer networks purely on the basis of qualitative arguments. They conclude that the number of training patterns should be 'at least several times larger than the network's capacity' (i.e. $P \gg W/K$). They refer to the work of Baum and Haussler (1989) who suggest that the appropriate number of training examples for multi-layer networks is given by:

$$P = \frac{W}{\epsilon}$$

where ϵ is an 'accuracy parameter' (the fraction of patterns from the test set which are incorrectly classified). Thus, for good generalisation, they suggest that the accuracy level might be 90%, corresponding to a value of 0.1 for ϵ, leading to a requirement of 'about 10 times as many training examples as ... weights in the network'.

All of the above can be summarised in the following statement:

A lower bound for the number of training patterns P is P = W.
A realistic upper bound might be P = 10W.

The number of examples which need to be acquired as part of the data collection process can therefore only be *estimated* in the first instance, since it requires a knowledge of the network architecture. Once the feasibility study is complete, however, the number of inputs I and the number of classes K should be known with a reasonable degree of confidence. The geometric mean $\sqrt{IK}$ can be used as a rough estimate for the number of hidden units J. The number of weights W in the network can then be calculated (see Equation (6.1)) and used as a first estimate of the *minimum* number of examples needed in the training set.

There is no discussion in the literature of similar issues for RBF networks. The free parameters of the first layer are set without reference to any labels: centre positions and widths depend purely on data distribution in input space; in some sense, there is no 'information cost' in determining these. The second layer can simply be treated as a single-layer network and hence the concept of network capacity could readily be applied here.

Data partitioning

As the reader will be aware by now, the process of developing a neural network solution requires not only a training set but also a test set and usually a validation set (when non-linear optimisation, as with a multi-layer perceptron, is used for weight adaptation). Ideally, the total number of examples should be divided equally between the training, validation and test sets (in the rest of this discussion, we will assume that both a training set and a validation set are required).

Thus the division of the overall data set ought to be in the ratios 1:1:1 for the training, validation and test sets. This can be very demanding when there is a significant cost attached to data collection since it means that the total number of examples must be three times that used simply for weight modification (the training set). When data is at a premium, it is possible to use cross-validation techniques which allow a greater proportion of the overall data set to be used as the training set, whilst still yielding reliable measures of generalisation. For n-fold cross-validation, there will be n different partitionings of the data set and hence n training experiments, the results of which will be averaged to give the overall performance. These techniques are explored in greater detail in the context of one of the case studies in Chapter 8.

Ambiguous inputs

Neural networks have no intrinsic difficulty dealing with data sets in which two or more significantly different input vectors map onto the same output vector. Indeed this can be *expected* to be the case for classification problems when data from the same class has a broad distribution in input space.

On the other hand, ambiguous inputs in the training data need to be identified at an early stage; this occurs when the same input vector appears more than once in the training dataset with different labels attached to it. If a neural network is trained with ambiguous input data without making any special allowances, it responds by learning the average of all the ambiguous target values for each output node. This will cause problems with test data and the ambiguous inputs should therefore be filtered out of the training set before training begins.

Input ambiguity should not be confused with noisy data. Noise in training data can lead to a neural network being required to associate several instances of this noisy input vector with different target vectors. For example, in a classification problem, the noise may cause the data point to lie just on the wrong side of the classification boundary. The advantage of the fact that neural network outputs are probability estimates (see Section 2.10) is that this would be indicated, for a two-class problem, by an output value just above or just below 0.5.

Noisy data is common to all pattern recognition problems. Real-world data is intrinsically noisy and hence the error rate on such data will never be zero. The aim of a properly trained neural network classifier is to arrive at a set of decision boundaries which will give good generalisation performance on the test set.

6.4   Data collection and data understanding

The collected data should preferably be stored in its 'raw' form, without any pre-processing, since pre-processing at this stage could inadvertently remove important aspects of the data. As the next chapter will emphasise, the choice of pre-processing algorithm is often a key step in the development of a neural computing application. However, it has to be the right form of pre-processing and, until this has been determined, no information should be discarded.

For some applications, it will also be important to keep records of the circumstances under which the data was collected. Such records are useful if, at a later stage in the project, there are doubts about the quality of some of the data; for example, in the course of training or testing the neural network, some data items appear to lead to unusually poor results. Checks can then be made to see whether these items were collected under unusual conditions. If there is a pattern to the distribution of suspect data (for example, most was collected on a Monday morning), the cause should be investigated and all data collected under similar circumstances should be regarded as questionable.

When the raw data has been collected and stored, it is useful to run simple data validity checks and to assess the data distribution before deciding whether sufficient data has been collected.

Data validity checks

Data validity checks can reveal any patently unacceptable data that, if retained for neural network training, could have a detrimental effect on the network weights (with an MLP, the weight update for the w_{ij} weights (see Appendix A) is directly proportional to the value of the input x_i; with an RBF network, erroneous inputs can cause centres to be placed in the wrong region of input space). An example of a simple validity check is a data range check: for example, if oven temperature data has been collected in degrees centigrade, values in the range 50 to 400 would be expected. A value of, say, -10, or 900, is clearly wrong.

Ideally, attempts should be made to check that the following conditions are met when the data is assembled into the input vectors:

1. all elements of the vectors are within the expected ranges;
2. all elements of the vectors are mutually consistent;
3. for a supervised learning application, the target vectors are consistent with the input vectors.

Assessing data distribution

As well as checking the validity of the data, it is equally important to ensure that the overall distribution of points within the training set is not flawed. There would be a problem if, for example, one of the data sources only ever returns a single value.

Histogram plots of the values of each input variable can also be very useful, for example in identifying outliers (abnormally large or abnormally small values) in the data set. The values of the variable under consideration should be ranked and then histogram plots of the distribution of these values should be constructed, firstly without the highest 10% and the lowest 10%, secondly without the highest 5% and the lowest 5%, thirdly without the highest 2% and

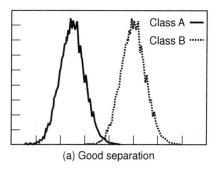
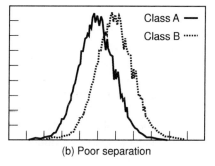

(a) Good separation   (b) Poor separation

Fig. 6.1 *Histogram plots of a variable x for two different classes.*

the lowest 2% and finally without the highest 1% and the lowest 1%. Values in the data set outside the range of the histogram plot should be identified for each of the plots; the position on the horizontal axis where they would be found will establish whether or not they are outliers. It is also helpful to see whether there are any significant changes in shape as the histogram plots gradually include more and more of the data values.

Once outliers have been identified, their occurrence can be noted for future reference or they can be removed if they correspond to erroneous values. For classification problems, a further set of plots can be constructed for each input variable, where the histograms for each class are shown on a single figure. This will give some indication of the discriminatory information contained in that variable alone. Figure 6.1 shows the type of plots which might be obtained for a two-class problem.

In Figure 6.1(a), there is a very clear separation between the values of the variable x for one class with respect to the values for the other class. Note that this is very much an idealised plot; if the separation were really as good as this, there would not be any need for training a neural network with several input variables: the class could be predicted accurately for nearly all cases simply on the basis of the value of x.

The right-hand plot is much more likely to be representative of real data, with only a marginal separation in the distribution of the values of x for the two classes. This is not to say, however, that x would not be an important input to a neural network. Consider, for example, the problem of assigning subjects either to a class 'low risk of heart attack' or to one of 'high risk of heart attack' on the basis of height measurement x_1 and weight measurement x_2. There is no doubt that there would be significant overlap between the height measurements for the two groups (as with Figure 6.1(b)). The neural network $f(x_1, x_2)$ would learn, however, that a combination of *small height* and *large weight*, for example, would lead to a significant risk of heart attack. Of course, this is a highly simplified description of a risk prediction problem by way of an illustration and a neural network trained to predict the risk of heart attack would take into account more than two prognostic factors.

Finally, note also that the variables are shown having near-Gaussian distributions. This is often *not* the case with real-world data. Also, the plots are relatively smooth, indicating that large numbers of examples were available for the problem under consideration. It is often the case that data is not as plentiful as one would wish and plotting histograms of the input variables will require careful selection of bin width: too large a value and it will be difficult to see any kind of shape to the distribution because of the coarseness of the quantisation; too small a value and there will be a risk of having bins with too little or no data.

Missing values

Real-world data sets often have missing values which it is impossible to retrieve later on. This is often the case in medical diagnostic systems when it is not always practical (or desirable) to run all possible tests on all patients. The subject of missing values is an important one in the statistics literature, and the book by Little and Rubin (1987), for example, is a detailed treatment of the subject. For the purposes of neural computing applications, we will consider three simple methods for imputation of missing values. All three methods make the assumption that values are missing at random.

The simplest method consists of replacing the missing value by its mean or median across the training set, μ_{TR}. (Note that this should *not* be the mean or median computed over the whole of the data set, since this would include information about the test set in the training set; note further that missing values in the validation and test sets are also replaced by μ_{TR}.) In a classification problem, the conditional mean or median can be used instead, i.e. the mean or median for the class to which the input vector belongs (again calculated using only the examples of that class in the training set).

The other two methods estimate the missing value, for an n-dimensional input vector, from knowledge of the other $n - 1$ input variables. In the first instance, the nearest neighbour in $(n - 1)$-dimensional space can be identified and the nth value for that input vector can be substituted for the missing element in the original input vector. (With a little thought, this approach can be extended to choosing the average of, or most common value in, K nearest neighbours rather than just the nearest neighbour.) Alternatively, a linear model or a neural network can be trained to *predict* the nth value given the set of $(n - 1)$-dimensional vectors as inputs—see, for example, Sharpe and Solly (1995). The database for this network is obviously the set of complete observations; once the network is trained, however, it can be used to impute the missing value from knowledge of the other $n - 1$ input variables.

Initially, the first method can be used to replace the missing value by its conditional mean or median when storing the input vectors in the database. (The database should also record which values are imputed rather than collected – it is important not to lose such information.) Of course, the first method can be used when the input vector has more than one missing element. Later on, the second and third methods can also be investigated when the stage of training the neural network for the application under consideration has been reached (see next chapter). These methods probably work best when one missing value has to be imputed. Their merit, with respect to the first method which is considerably simpler, can be evaluated retrospectively by comparing the generalisation performance of three sets of neural networks *trained under exactly the same conditions* save for the fact that the missing values in the input vectors have been generated by one of the three different methods.

Partitioning data

Partitioning is the process of dividing the data into the training, validation and test sets. The overall data set should contain sufficient data (and a suitable data distribution) to ensure that the network can learn the non-linear mapping f between the input and output variables x and y over the whole range of operation.

In the first instance, data should be allocated *randomly* between the training, validation and test sets, if possible in the ratios 1:1:1 (see Section 6.3 above). This principle should be applied with care, however. Consider a medical signal analysis problem, for example, in which the aim is to classify electrocardiogram (ECG) waveforms into 'normal' or 'abnormal' classes. Assume that a balanced database of 3000 input vectors has been assembled from a group of 9 patients. Assume further that a label (0 for normal, 1 for abnormal) has been assigned by an expert clinician to each of the input vectors. (As will be made clear in the next chapter, the input vectors are likely to be a set of features, describing the shape of the waveform in this case, rather than the raw data, but this does not affect the argument presented here.) If the approach suggested above for randomly allocating the input data is followed, training, validation and test sets, each of 1000 examples will be constructed. The problem with this approach is that the data from all 9 patients would appear *in all three data sets*. Strictly speaking, waveforms from the patients in the test set should *not* appear in the training set or they would play a part in the training of the neural network model. A preliminary division should therefore take place for problems of this type *before* data partitioning: 3 patients should have their entire data kept back for the test set (with again approximately equal numbers of normal and abnormal waveforms) before the data from the other 6 is used to create the training and validation sets by random allocation of the input vectors from these patients.

It should be noted, finally, that this strict partitioning can be relaxed when it is known (from data analysis) that the intra-class variability for one subject is greater than the inter-subject variability. This is the case for the electroencephalogram (EEG) data used for one of the case studies in Chapter 8.

7
DESIGN, TRAINING AND TESTING OF THE PROTOTYPE

7.1 Introduction

Neural computing application development usually proceeds by an iterative process of design refinement. There are two reasons for this:

1. the full scope and complexity of the problem may not be immediately apparent although benchmark results using linear regression or a linear classifier should have given some indication of these (see the end of Chapter 4 and especially the case studies in the next chapter);
2. it is difficult to predict the performance of a neural network and the way it could vary when changing design parameters such as neural network size and choice of input features.

As a result of this, it is not possible to draw up a full design specification initially, and some design decisions can only be resolved by experimentation. Clearly, there is a balance between what can be reliably specified in the initial design and what must be left to be resolved by experiment. This balance will vary from one project to another and according to prior experience with neural computing.

Depending on the application, it may be appropriate to use a mix of technologies for different parts of the problem rather than neural networks for all of them. As with a conventional IT project, the major system components need to be identified at the outset and their function should then be specified as accurately as possible. In some applications, major components can be sub-divided into simpler functions which can be implemented by separate neural networks. Such a design may be more effective than one with a single, large, complex neural network.

7.2 Overview of design

Figure 7.1 shows the neural network and related sub-components in a neural computing application. There are no hard and fast rules for many aspects of

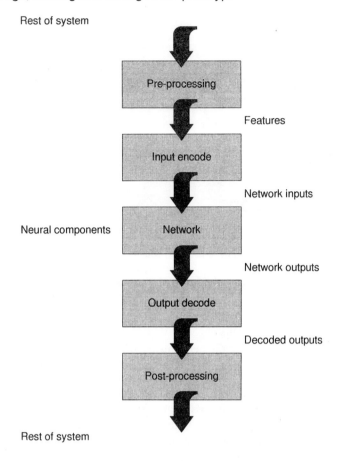

Fig. 7.1 *The components of a neural computing sub-system.*

neural network design. It involves experimental optimisation, which should be performed with a clear understanding of the issues and objectives of the project.

The following issues need to be considered with care:

- pre-processing;
- input/output encoding;
- selection of neural network type and architecture;
- training the prototype;
- testing the prototype.

The rest of this chapter is concerned with an examination of each of these in turn.

It was made clear in Chapter 4 that the first requirement for a successful neural computing application is that prior knowledge about the problem domain should be applied to the design of the neural network. An understanding of the data, and the processes that generate the data, should direct the choice of pre-processing method; in practice, this often means the selection of suitable features to be presented to the network. Similarly, as discussed below, a knowledge of the properties of the data can help with the construction of appropriate input and output encodings.

7.3 Pre-processing

Neural networks very rarely operate directly on the raw data. A possible exception to this is time-series prediction (Weigend and Gershenfeld, 1993) in which n consecutive data samples are applied at the input of a neural network, the output of which is a prediction of the $(n + 1)$th sample (one-step ahead prediction). Note that, even here, prior knowledge may be required to choose the value of n; it is no use, for example, choosing a value of six or less when the data has a seven-day periodicity.

With most types of applications other than time-series prediction, there is usually an initial pre-processing procedure applied to the raw data. For many applications, this procedure is a very important part of the neural computing solution. Almost invariably, it is a dimensionality reduction technique since a network with fewer inputs will have fewer free parameters, in which case the learning procedure (minimisation of output error) with a finite data set is more likely to yield a properly determined network with good generalisation properties. The reduction in input dimensionality is usually achieved either by extracting features from the raw data or directly by Principal Components Analysis (PCA). Each of these is now considered in turn.

Feature extraction

The first case study in Chapter 8 is concerned with analysing the electroencephalogram (the EEG, which is a record of the brain's electrical activity) during sleep. Since neural networks are static pattern analysers, the EEG is segmented into one-second sections. A neural network is then trained to assign these one-second segments to one of three classes, according to sleep state (see Chapter 8 for a more detailed description). With a sampling rate of 128 Hz, there are 128 samples of raw EEG signal in each one-second segment. There are two reasons why the raw EEG could *not* be used as the input to the neural network: in the first instance, a prohibitively large number of examples would be required to populate the 128-dimensional input space and so the network would very much be under-determined; secondly, prior knowledge tells us that the discriminatory information in the EEG is not in the time domain but in the *frequency* domain. The dominant frequencies in the EEG change according to sleep state (with a shift towards lower frequencies as the depth of sleep increases). We therefore need to apply a dimensionality-reducing frequency-domain transformation as a pre-processing step.

The most obvious method to use would have been the Fast Fourier Transform, which is a computationally efficient method for calculating the amplitude spectrum (or the power spectrum) of a sampled signal. The 128 time domain samples from one-second segments of EEG sampled at 128 Hz would produce 64 coefficients from 0 to 64 Hz according to the following equation:

$$F(k) = \sum_{n=0}^{N-1} f(n) \exp\left(-j\frac{2\pi nk}{N}\right)$$

where $F(k)$ is the kth frequency coefficient, $f(n)$ is the nth time domain sample in the original N-sample window (i.e. $N = 128$ here) and $j = \sqrt{-1}$. Details of the Fast Fourier Transform and how to calculate it are given in most Digital Signal Processing books (see Rabiner and Gold, 1975, for example).

Although the set of $F(k)$ values (or more exactly, their modulus if we are interested in the amplitude spectrum) provides a frequency-domain representation, it is still unsuitable because of its high dimensionality. One approach might be to group the coefficients together in order to produce a coarser (and hence lower dimensionality) representation, for example by averaging groups of eight consecutive coefficients together in order to obtain an 8-dimensional input vector. We can improve on this, however, by applying further prior knowledge about the sleep EEG. We know that the *dominant* frequencies vary according to sleep state and we can therefore employ techniques originally developed for speech processing (Makhoul, 1975) based on all-pole auto-regressive models of the segmented signal (Pardey *et al.*, 1996a). A model with 10 coefficients allows us to track the location and 'sharpness' of four dominant frequencies. This gives us a low-dimensional representation which encodes the information of interest and should therefore lead to a neural computing solution with good generalisation properties.

The second case study presented in Chapter 8 is concerned with predicting whether or not a female subject is diabetic, given the values of seven physiological parameters for that subject. In this case, the input data is a set of features and hence there is no need for a pre-processing step. This is typical of many prognosis problems, whether in medicine or in condition monitoring. Another example of a similar medical prognostic problem is the prediction of whether a woman is likely to relapse after breast cancer has been diagnosed and a primary tumour has been removed. At the time that the tumour is removed, information about the size of the tumour, the number of nodes and other biochemical indicators are available as prognostic indicators. These can then be used as the inputs to a neural network classifier (probability of relapse within a fixed period of time, say three or five years—see Tarassenko *et al.*, 1996) or for regression analysis (prediction of time to relapse—see Ripley *et al.*, 1997).

Image analysis is a subject on its own and there are many papers in the neural network literature devoted to this topic. A note of caution must be sounded about many of the early papers as they report work in which the raw image data is applied directly as the input to the neural network. Since there are thousands of pixels in any image (unless pixels have been grouped together to provide a much coarser representation), the network has thousands of inputs and an even larger number of weights, leading to a hugely under-determined network for which the number of free parameters is several orders of magnitude greater than the number of training patterns. The results presented in such papers may at first sight appear to vindicate the approach, but it is *not* the case that an input–output mapping of the form $y = f(x)$ has been learnt. Rather the images from the training set have been stored in the weights in an *ad hoc* fashion and the 'trained' network acts as an approximate template matching architecture when processing test data. An exception to this type of behaviour is the work of LeCun *et al.* (1990) on recognition of zip codes, in which the first stage of neural processing acts directly on small patches of the raw image data. This is a valid approach in this case because the neural network is a highly constrained network (weights are only allowed to take on a limited set of values) which therefore has very few degrees of freedom. Such a network effectively acts as a feature extraction stage and is similar to the convolution masks which are used in conventional image processing.

Feature extraction is therefore an inevitable part of image analysis with a neural network. For example, if it is required to find regions of unhealthy tissue in X-ray mammograms of women at risk of breast cancer, features relating to the distribution of pixel values within the region of interest, its texture, the edge strengths of any closed contour and the contrast with respect to neighbouring regions would represent an appropriate feature set (Tarassenko *et al.*, 1995).

Dimensionality reduction using Principal Components Analysis

When the input data is high-dimensional and there are no obvious features which can be extracted from it, the input dimensionality must nevertheless be reduced in order to limit the number of free parameters in the network (since this is mainly determined by the number of inputs – see Section 6.3) and obtain good generalisation with finite data sets. In these cases, Principal Components Analysis (PCA) is a suitable technique to apply for dimensionality reduction.

With PCA, new variables are defined which are linear combinations of all the input variables. As explained in Bishop (1995), for example, the first step in PCA is to calculate the data covariance matrix Σ:

$$\Sigma = \sum_{p=1}^{P} (x^p - \mu)(x^p - \mu)^T$$

where P is the number of vectors in the training set and μ is the mean vector for this data set. The eigenvectors and eigenvalues of Σ are then calculated and

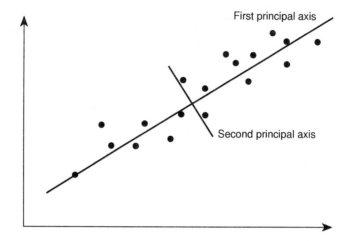

Fig. 7.2 *A simple illustration of PCA on two-dimensional data.*

ordered. For a reduction in dimensionality from n to m (where, usually, $m \ll n$), the eigenvectors corresponding to the m largest eigenvalues are retained and the input vectors x^p are then projected onto these eigenvectors in order to give a new set of input vectors in m-dimensional space.

Figure 7.2 gives a two-dimensional illustration of PCA. As can be clearly seen from the distribution of the points, most of the variation in the data is along the first principal axis. In order to encode this two-dimensional data as one variable, each point is projected onto the first principal axis and the co-ordinate along this axis becomes the one-dimensional input variable.

7.4 Input/output encoding

For a network to be able to generalise correctly, an important criterion is that the training data should be coded in a form which allows interpolation. This is explained in Figure 7.3 which shows a 2-D representation of possible solution 'surfaces' arising out of different input codings. The third plot shows that it becomes much easier to fit a surface to training data for which the input coding has been optimised.

There are many potential applications of neural networks in the fields of commerce and finance, where there are many types of data available, not all of which are numerical: some may be symbolic codes or free-form text. Before non-numerical data can be used by a neural network, it has to be transformed into meaningful numbers. However, if arbitrary numerical codes are assigned to text strings, for example 'London' = 1, 'Edinburgh' = 2, and 'Sheffield' = 3, this would imply that Sheffield is 'greater than' Edinburgh, and Edinburgh greater than London. A more meaningful approach to processing non-numerical data is

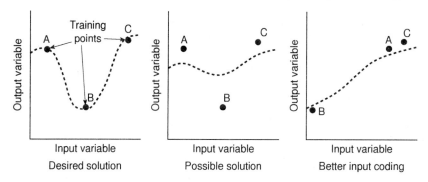

Fig. 7.3 *Importance of choice of input coding for an MLP.*

to assign numerical values derived according to an appropriate distance metric. For example, data elements with similar characteristics should be represented as close together in the input space of the neural network, while elements with very different characteristics should be widely separated.

The rest of this section provides an overview of techniques for converting various data types to an appropriate representation for neural computing. The techniques discussed below apply to both the inputs and outputs of a neural network, although they are most widely used for input encoding.

Categorical variables

A categorical variable is a variable that can belong to one of a number of discrete categories, for example red, green or blue. Categorical variables are usually encoded using a 1-out-of-n coding where, if there are n values, n variables are used such that the relevant unit (for example, that corresponding to 'red') is set to 1 while the rest ('blue' and 'green') are set to 0. In this example, there are therefore three possible input codes: $(1, 0, 0)$, $(0, 1, 0)$ and $(0, 0, 1)$. Binary categorical variables (usually Yes/No) are an exception to this form of coding: they are simply encoded as 0 or 1 in a single input.

It is also sometimes suggested that categories could be encoded as a single input by numbering the categories (for example, red = 1, green = 2, blue = 3), and then dividing by the number of categories. This would encode the values as $1/n$, $2/n$, etc. This type of encoding is to be avoided as it imposes an ordering on the values of the variable which does not exist and would therefore provide misleading information to the neural network.

Continuous variables

For continuous variables, it is usually sufficient to apply each variable directly to the input of the neural network. The variables will often have dynamic ranges which differ by orders of magnitude, however, and this suggests that a suitable normalisation should be applied so that the transformed variables all cover the same range. The most appropriate transformation is the zero-mean unit-variance transformation which is a *linear* transformation applied to each input variable x_i independently. As shown in Section 2.12, the mean μ_i and the variance σ_i^2 of the variable are first of all calculated over all the training examples. The normalised value of x_i is then given by:

$$x_i^* = \frac{x_i - \mu_i}{\sigma_i}$$

Once the parameters of the transformation, μ_i and σ_i^2, have been computed, they are applied to all input patterns presented to the network, whether from the training, validation or test set, so that all patterns are given the same normalisation.

The zero-mean unit-variance transformation is not required at the input of an MLP as, in principle, the weights should be able to adapt to the different dynamic ranges of the input. When input variables have very large magnitudes, however, it may not be possible to train the network since the weighted summation $\sum w_{ij} x_i$ to some of the hidden units, with the original random weight set, may turn out to be very large, for example > 10.0 (or < -10.0 for negative inputs with a large magnitude). It is easy to show, for the standard sigmoid function of Figure 2.5, that $y_j > 0.98$ when $\sum w_{ij} x_i \geq 4.0$ and $y_j < 0.02$ when $\sum w_{ij} x_i \leq -4.0$. Thus, if $\sum w_{ij} x_i$ is > 10.0 or < -10.0, y_j will have a value very close to 1.0 or 0.0. The problem is that it *will remain at this value* since the derivative of the sigmoid activation function is zero for very positive (or very negative) values of $\sum w_{ij} x_i$ (see Figure 2.5) and the weight updates are proportional to this derivative (see Appendix A). This is the phenomenon of 'stuck units'. Even if the initial weight set is adjusted in order to compensate for this, learning will still proceed very slowly as many iterations will be required before a final weight set with a large enough dynamic range is obtained.

With RBF networks, the zero-mean unit-variance transformation is *essential* as the Euclidean distance metric is used to compute the activation of the hidden units. As also discussed in Section 2.12, the Euclidean distance metric implicitly assigns more weight to input variables with large dynamic ranges than to those with small ranges. The zero-mean unit-variance transformation is therefore used to prevent some variables from dominating the Euclidean distance calculations simply because they vary over a much wider range than the others.

Ordinal variables

Ordinal variables are continuous variables (which may have been discretised) but have a natural ordering. For example, a person's weight may be given as being between 8 and $8\frac{1}{2}$ stone, another one as being between $11\frac{1}{2}$ and 12 stone.

Such data can simply be transformed directly into corresponding values of a continuous variable.

Periodic variables

Occasionally variables have periodic values, for example the day of the week or the time of day. With periodic variables, the highest and lowest values of the range are conceptually adjacent, hence a periodic variable can be encoded by transforming it into an angle, taking the sine and cosine of the angle and applying it to two input units.

Choosing appropriate input/output codes—Application I

The conversion of English text to elementary speech sounds (phonemes) is a medium-sized problem which was used as a benchmark for the evaluation of MLPs in the early days of neural computing (Sejnowski and Rosenberg, 1987). The conventional approach to this problem is to use a look-up table (> 100 kbytes) to store the phonetic transcription of common and irregular words *and* phonological rules for the rest of the vocabulary. With the neural network approach known as NETtalk, the text is applied to the input of an MLP in binary format using a 7-letter window (in other words, the current letter at the centre of the window and a context of three letters, or punctuation marks, either side of the central letter—see Figure 7.4). In the original work, a simple 1-out-of-n input coding was used to encode each of the seven input characters. Since there are 26 letters in the English alphabet and two punctuation marks and a space were also allowed, this gave a 1-out-of-29 coding with the letter A encoded as a 1 followed by 28 zeros, the letter B encoded as a 0 followed by a 1 followed by 27 zeros and so on. Since this is a very sparse binary coding (there are only seven 1s out of the 203 bits which make up any input pattern), an input representation with very high dimensionality is allowable in this very specific case.

An output coding was constructed to represent the articulatory features of spoken speech (details are given in Sejnowski and Rosenberg, 1987). A 203-80-26 network was then assembled and trained to learn the text-to-speech mapping. The percentage of correct phonemes, after learning, was given as 95% on the training set and 78% on a test set selected by the authors. When NETtalk was re-implemented as NETspeak for British English as opposed to American English (McCulloch *et al.*, 1987), a 90% score was obtained on the training data set; however, it was noticed that it was most often the *key* phoneme which was wrong in a word and only 33% of the *words* in the training set were transcribed with no phoneme errors.

The reason for this poor performance was investigated and it was concluded that performance could be improved significantly if *a priori* information was incorporated into the neural network solution. It is obvious that the MLP is able

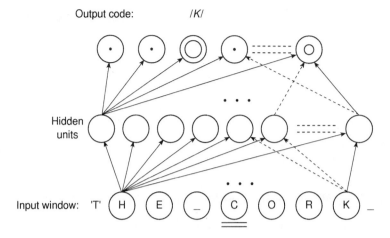

Output code: /K/

Hidden units

Input window: 'T' H E _ C O R K _

Fig. 7.4 *MLP architecture for text-to-speech synthesis.*

to derive a non-linear mapping from input to output although the input coding does not represent in any way how letters are grouped in written English (for example, the fact that the letters t and h are very often next to each other is not taken into account in the input coding). An input encoding was therefore constructed which captured some of the features of English text by constraining the Hamming distances[1] between letters to reflect the cost of confusing them (for a more detailed explanation, see Tombs, 1989). When this optimised input coding was used with NETspeak, there was indeed a very significant improvement in the percentage of words transcribed with no phoneme errors, from 33% to 52% and from 37% to 54% on a listener test. It should be noted, when assessing these results, that the best rule-based system available only scores 61% on the listener test, primarily because of the limitations of the hardware formant synthesiser used for speech output. Thus the performance of an MLP with optimised input coding became comparable to that of a rule-based system developed over many years.

Choosing appropriate input/output codes – Application II

Consider now a hypothetical application in which a major lending library wishes to study the reading habits of its customers to assist in publicity, or for defining its acquisitions policy. Typically, the data would consist of two types of record: a customer record, containing the customer's name, age, occupation and other relevant personal details, as well as a transaction record containing the name of the book, the dates when it was borrowed and returned, and the name of the borrower.

---

[1] For a definition of Hamming distance, see Section 2.20.

There are a number of generic issues which would arise when processing the customer and transaction data:

- fields with a large number of options should be grouped sensibly. For example, 'occupation' may have hundreds of options, and these should be grouped to reduce the number of inputs to the neural network and hence improve its ability to generalise. For example, customers working in banking, accountancy, finance or the insurance industry could be grouped under a single heading called 'finance';
- addresses are difficult to encode, but if demography is considered to be important, postcodes could be encoded by using, for example, grid reference co-ordinates, so that adjacent post regions would be close together in input space;
- numerical fields such as the Dewey Decimal categorisation of library books should be treated with caution. There is no significance, with this categorisation, in the fact that one code is greater than another. A possible way to deal with this would be to group the classifications, and form a pie-chart or histogram reflecting the number of transactions within each group. The numerical values of the pie-chart fraction could then be used as one of the neural network's inputs;
- statistics on frequency and volume of use over a given period of time (a month, for example) could also provide valuable information on the reading habits of the library's customers.

If all of the above data was concatenated into an n-dimensional feature vector (after each variable had been normalised as discussed earlier), a Kohonen feature map could then be trained on large numbers of vectors in order to try and visualise whether there were any natural groupings (i.e. clusters) within the data. If the dimensionality was too high ($n \gg 10$), then it might be more advisable to use sub-sets of the available features and look for clusters in these first.

7.5   Selection of neural network type

As already mentioned in an earlier chapter, this book focuses on just one unsupervised learning technique, the Kohonen map. There are alternative (non-neural) algorithms such as Sammon's mapping which is briefly described in Chapter 9. The rest of this chapter concentrates on MLP and RBF networks for supervised learning. Kohonen networks (and associated pathologies) are covered in detail in the case studies of Chapter 8.

The neural computing research literature is rich in papers which propose alternative network architectures but, in the main, these are simply variations on the existing MLP and RBF architectures. For this reason, this book is focusing on these two types of networks for supervised learning and this section presents a discussion of their relative merits, which should help to decide which is most appropriate for the regression or classification problem under consideration.

The case studies will show that RBF networks and MLPs produce similar levels of generalisation, although MLPs tend to out-perform RBF networks by a small amount. The main advantage of RBF networks is usually perceived to be the much lower training times in comparison to the full non-linear optimisation of the error back-propagation algorithm used with MLPs. As described in Chapter 2, training an RBF network consists of two phases: the position of the centres in input space is first of all determined using unsupervised clustering (usually the K-means algorithm); the widths are then set using one of a number of heuristics. In the second phase, the hidden layer representation becomes the input to the second layer which is trained independently. Since this is a linear optimisation task, it can be performed using matrix pseudo-inverse techniques or the LMS algorithm. This two-phase approach is very fast but classification results tend to be slightly worse than with an MLP. The K-means algorithm sets the free parameters of the first layer purely according to the distribution of the training data in input space: any class information is ignored. If class labels *are* used and the centre positions are adjusted using gradient descent (adapting the error back-propagation algorithm to the RBF architecture), it can be shown that the classification performance of an RBF network is almost identical to that of an MLP (Tarassenko and Roberts, 1994). The improvement in training times, however, no longer obtains and so we will not consider this option any further.

RBF networks do offer other significant advantages in that the hidden layer representation is much more accessible. The centres in the hidden layer can be chosen to be the units in a Kohonen feature map and hence any clustering of the input vectors should become apparent on the trained feature map.

The hidden layer representation of the RBF network has one other advantage: it can be used as a *novelty detector* on test patterns, indicating whether the network is interpolating, as it should be, or extrapolating, in which case no confidence can be attached to the output classification. (The latter case is indicated by having very low activities throughout the hidden layer as the test vector is outside the boundaries of the training data used to set the centre positions and widths.) It can thus be argued that the hidden-layer representation of an RBF network trained with the two-phase approach is much more powerful than that of an MLP, and this can therefore be traded off against a slight degradation in classification performance. The relative importance of these issues will depend on the application.

7.6   Selection of neural network architecture

The number of *layers* required in an MLP is no longer an issue. In Lippmann's early review paper (1987), it was suggested that a three-layer MLP (since we count layers of *weights*, this corresponds to an *i-j-k-l* MLP with w_{ij}, w_{jk}

and w_{kl} weights) was required to form any arbitrary complex decision boundary and separate meshed classes. This was constructed from geometrical arguments, however, for MLPs with *hard-limiting* non-linearities. As already mentioned in Chapter 2, a two-layer MLP with sigmoid non-linearities can approximate any function with arbitrary accuracy (the property of universal approximation) although theory cannot predict *how many* hidden units would be required for a given problem in order to obtain a given accuracy. The problem therefore reduces to the choice of number of hidden units, as discussed in Section 2.9 of Chapter 2 and further in Section 7.7 below.

The same property of universal approximation has been shown to hold for RBF networks with one hidden layer (Park and Sandberg, 1991). The size of an RBF network is therefore determined by the number of centres in the hidden layer. As the dimensionality of the problem increases, the number of centres needed to cover the input space rises very rapidly. In practice, this limits RBF networks to problems having a small number of inputs, though this limitation can be alleviated by suitable pre-processing. For example, Principal Components Analysis can be used to reduce the effective dimensionality of the problem as shown earlier in this chapter.

7.7   Training and testing the prototype

During the training of the prototype, a series of training runs will take place until the optimal architecture and the 'optimal' set of weights is obtained. The procedures required to reach this stage are now described in detail for an MLP classifier. An equivalent set of procedures would be adopted for an RBF network except that training an RBF network, as pointed out in the comparison between the two types of networks in Chapter 2, is simpler because the second phase in the two-phase strategy is only one of *linear* optimisation; a validation set is therefore not required since there is only one (global) minimum for the given hidden layer parameters. In any case, the case studies of the next chapter will provide ample illustration of the training procedures for *both* types of networks.

The selection of an optimal MLP as part of the training procedure is now described in detail. There are four main tasks involved in training and testing a prototype MLP classifier:

1. partitioning the data into training, validation and test sets;
2. training the MLP (until the stopping criterion is met);
3. selecting the optimal network;
4. testing the trained network using the test set.

It is important to perform multiple training runs because of the nature of the training algorithm: with non-linear optimisation, there are many different local minima in weight space. Hence different random initialisations will produce different weight sets when training is stopped, each corresponding to a different local minimum. (With an RBF network, different choices for the prototype vectors at the start of the K-means algorithm will give different sets of centres, but for each of these there will be one optimal set of weights for the second layer which can be determined by matrix inversion.)

As an illustration, we will assume that there will be ten runs[2], each with different random weight initialisations, for each value of j, the number of hidden units in the I-j-K network. The pseudo-code for ten runs for each value of j is given below:

1. partition the data into training, validation and test sets;
2. for $(j = 1; j <= j_{max}; j++)$
   {

       for (run = 1; run <= 10; run++)
       {

           initialise the weights;
           train MLP and continue training until the stopping criterion is met (min. classification error on the validation set, $(e_{val})_{min}$, has been reached);
           save value of $(e_{val})_{min}$ and corresponding weight set;

       }

   }
3. select the optimal network on the basis of the lowest value of $(e_{val})_{min}$ and retrieve the corresponding weight set;
4. test the optimal network using the test set.

We will now consider tasks 2 to 4 in detail.

Initialising the weights

When training an MLP with the error back-propagation algorithm, the first step for any training run is to initialise the weights in both layers by setting each one to a small random number (typically in the range -0.01 to $+0.01$). As multiple training runs will be performed, the random number generator must be configured to give a different sequence of random numbers each time. This is usually achieved by specifying a different 'seed'. (As indicated in Chapter 3, it is useful to store the value of the seed as reproducing the results of any experiment may be required.)

All of the initial w_{ij} and w_{jk} weight values *must* be close to zero. If their magnitudes are too large, learning will be very slow or may not proceed at all because the activations of the sigmoid units will be close to or on the saturated part of the sigmoid function, where the derivative is nearly zero. A very large change in weights is required to make a small change in the output of such a

---

[2]This is an arbitrary choice and the number could be higher in practice.

unit, and the learning process, which relies on *small* changes to the weights, will be extremely slow. In the extreme, the phenomenon of 'stuck units' (described earlier in Section 7.4) will occur, whereby a hidden unit y_j or output unit y_k will remain stuck at a value close to either 1.0 or 0.0.

Training the network

The error back-propagation algorithm is an iterative algorithm. Input vectors need to be presented to the network repeatedly, and in random order if the weights are to be updated after the presentation of each pattern. The output error E is measured and gradient descent is used to adjust the weights so as to reduce this error by a small amount.

For each training pattern presented during an epoch, the network output is computed using the current weight set and compared to the target output for that input pattern. This gives rise to the squared error at the output, E, which is used to calculate the Δw_{jk} weight updates and then back-propagation of this error (the δ terms in the equations below, previously defined in Equations (2.9) and (2.11) of Section 2.8) allows the Δw_{ij} weight updates to be calculated. If a momentum term is added, the weight update equations, already given in Chapter 2, become:

$$\Delta w_{jk} = w_{jk}(t+1) - w_{jk}(t) = -\eta \delta_k y_j + \alpha(w_{jk}(t) - w_{jk}(t-1))$$
$$\Delta w_{ij} = w_{ij}(t+1) - w_{ij}(t) = -\eta \delta_j y_i + \alpha(w_{ij}(t) - w_{ij}(t-1))$$

The learning rate η and the momentum parameter α in the above equations need to be set. Usually, the choice of these values is not critical provided that η is less than 0.1, when momentum is being used. Typically, η will be between 0.01 and 0.1 and α will be set to a value between 0.5 and 0.99.

There are two alternative methods, batch and sequential learning, for applying these equations to the task of training an MLP. With *batch learning*, the weight updates are averaged over all the training patterns, for each epoch. Thus:

$$\Delta w' = \frac{1}{P} \sum_{p=1}^{P} \Delta w$$

$\Delta w'$ is only applied to w at the end of each epoch. With *sequential learning*, the weights are updated after the presentation of *each pattern*. Although this is a stochastic learning procedure with no guarantee of convergence (except under restricted conditions − see Bishop, 1995), in practice sequential learning is almost always used in preference to batch learning.

Although stochastic learning theory requires that the order of presentation should be random throughout training, experience suggests that the input vectors should be randomised once and for all before training commences. Once this randomisation has taken place, keeping to the same order of presentation throughout training produces smoother curves when the training and validation classification errors are plotted against the number of iterations, or epochs, to monitor the progress of training. (An epoch, as defined in Chapter 2, is an iteration through the entire training set.)

When using sequential learning (updating the weights after the presentation of each pattern), it is important *not* to adapt the w_{jk} weights before computing the Δw_{ij} weight updates (which depend on the w_{jk} values through the δ_j term). The error back-propagation algorithm is an efficient mathematical procedure for updating *all* the weights in a network based on a single measurement of the output squared error. Inherent in the use of partial derivatives is the assumption that all other parameters are held constant and hence all the weights in the network must be adapted at the same time.

Stopping criterion

When the neural network is being trained, the weight set is adapted in order to minimise the mean square error (MSE) over the training set. Ideally, parameter optimisation would be based on the criterion which we wish to minimise (*classification* error rate) but there is no principled method for achieving this at the moment. A compromise is to continue mimimising the training MSE using the error back-propagation algorithm but to monitor the classification error rate on the validation set in order to decide when to stop training. (If the validation MSE is used instead, it turns out that it will make little or no difference in practice (Tarassenko *et al.*, 1996). In general, training continues for longer and the minimum obtained on the validation set may well be less pronounced.)

Thus the progress of learning is followed by continuously monitoring the classification error on the validation set, e_{val}. This is calculated over all the patterns in the validation set at the end of each training epoch. If e_{val} is plotted as a function of the number of epochs, the behaviour which should be observed (see Figure 7.5) is one in which it decreases rapidly at first, in very much the same way as the classification error on the training set, e_{tr} (also computed at the end of each epoch, using the same weight set on all of the training patterns).

Eventually, e_{val} stops decreasing or even starts to rise whilst e_{tr} continues to decrease. It is at this point that training should be stopped and the network's weights saved. In practice, training is continued for a few more epochs to ensure that the validation error has indeed reached its minimum value or that its rate of change is close to zero. There may be a small amount of oscillation from epoch to epoch but the minimum validation error, $(e_{\text{val}})_{\text{min}}$, should be taken to be the first minimum or the 'knee' of the curve, as shown in Figure 7.5, and it is the corresponding weight set which should be regarded as the optimal weight set for this network configuration and this choice of initial weights.

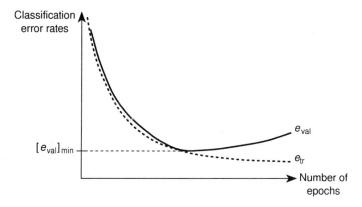

Fig. 7.5 *Plots of training and validation classification error rates during training.*

Selecting the optimal network

As should be clear from the pseudo-code, step 3 is used to identify the optimal I-j-K configuration on the basis of the lowest value of $(e_{val})_{min}$ obtained during the training runs of step 2. This procedure can of course be adapted to provide the *m* best networks, as opposed to simply *the* optimal network, by modifying step 3 as follows:

> 3. select the *m* best networks on the basis of the *m* lowest values of $(e_{val})_{min}$ and retrieve the corresponding weight sets;

Finally, in cases where data is scarce, an outer loop can be introduced so that different partitionings of the available data into training, validation and test sets are created for each loop. This is the basis of *cross-validation* techniques which are considered in detail in the context of the second case study in the next chapter.

Testing the trained neural network(s)

The test set is a part of the collected data that is set aside to test how well a trained neural network generalises. The generalisation performance is assessed by presenting the previously unseen patterns of the test set either to the optimal network or the *m* best networks as determined above. In the latter case, the generalisation performance can be assessed as the average of the classification performance of each of the *m* best networks. This is the simplest form of a *committee of networks* and often the most effective.

A common mistake is to select the *m* best networks on the basis of the test set performance. *This is not a fair test of generalisation performance* as the test set wrongly becomes part of the optimisation procedure. The only principled method with which to determine which sets of weights to retain is by selecting the networks which perform best on the validation set, as described above. The weights are then 'frozen' and the networks are then assessed on data not previously seen.

The confusion probably arises out of the fact that the test set used to evaluate generalisation performance is in many ways an artificial test set, in that it comes with a correct set of labels as for the training and validation sets. In real life, the answers will not be known for the test cases (for example, when a new food item is placed inside a microwave oven controlled by a neural network, it does not usually come with a label indicating how long it should be cooked for under the prevailing conditions). Of course, if the operating conditions change over time and the test data is significantly different from the training data, the neural network will have to be re-trained but this will have to be re-done from scratch with all of the data being re-partitioned into training, validation and test sets.

7.8 From prototype to deliverable system

Once generalisation performance on a genuinely independent test set has been shown to be satisfactory, the software from the trained prototype is ready to be transferred to the deliverable system, as discussed in the last section of Chapter 3. There are two important requirements for maintaining confidence in the operation of the neural network at the core of the deliverable system:

1. Some estimate of the error at the output of the trained neural network should be provided. Errors arise as a result of noise on the input data, uncertainty in the weights and noise on the target values (for a regression problem). The whole subject of error bars is growing in importance within the field of neural computing (Williams *et al.*, 1995; Tibshirani, 1996; Heskes, 1997; Townsend and Tarassenko, 1997). A simple strategy to adopt would be to monitor the variance of the estimates produced by the m best networks (where m may be set equal to 10, for example). If the variance on new data remains similar to that observed on the training data, then confidence in the output values will be maintained.

2. The neural network should never be allowed to extrapolate, i.e. it should never be used to analyse input vectors which are outside the boundaries of the training data in input space. This requires the *novelty* of the test vectors to be monitored (Roberts and Tarassenko, 1994; Bishop, 1994; Tarassenko *et al.*, 1995; Nairac *et al.*, 1997a).

7.9 Common problems in training and/or testing the prototype

We end this chapter with a short section on the problems which are commonly encountered when training or testing a neural network. Most of the 'pathologies' described below will also be explored in the context of the case studies in the next chapter.

Poor training performance

In some cases, the training error will remain consistently high as the network fails to learn a mapping from x, the set of input vectors, to y, the output data. There are several possible reasons for this:

Incorrect choice of problem

The problem under consideration is not the type of problem that a neural network can learn. There is no relationship between x and y; an example of this would be an attempt to predict the weather from sunrise/sunset times and the day of the week.

Wrong set of features

In this case, there is a relationship between the input signal or image and the output data, but the wrong set of features has been chosen to characterise the former. This would arise, for example, when trying to determine sleep state from the raw EEG, when it is in the frequency domain that the discriminatory information is found (see Section 7.3 in this chapter).

Stuck units

This problem has been discussed on a couple of occasions in this chapter, in the section on normalisation of continuous variables in Section 7.4 and again in Section 7.7. It is a problem of initialisation, caused either by choosing an initial set of random weights whose magnitudes are too large or by failing to normalise the input variables properly. The problem can be detected easily enough by observing the values of the hidden and output units after initialisation but prior to the start of learning. Ideally, they should all be close to 0.5; if any of them are near 0.0 or 1.0, then a new set of random weights should be generated or the normalisation of the input variables should be checked.

Poor generalisation performance

Here we are considering cases for which the error on the test set is unacceptably high despite the fact that the error on the training set was minimised during learning and reached a reasonably low value by the end of training. This is not an uncommon phenomenon in the first stages of prototype design, training and testing. However, most of the pathologies described below can be put right; as stated in the introduction to this chapter, the development of neural computing applications is an iterative process.

Insufficient number of training patterns

This is an issue which has been discussed at length in Chapter 6. If there is insufficient information for the network weights to be determined properly, the training patterns will be 'learnt' rather than the underlying relationship between x and y. This phenomenon may also be indicated by a validation error which is significantly higher than the training error, although this will depend on the data distribution within the validation set compared with that in the training set.

Over-fitting

This problem is one of model order. The complexity of the network (which is determined by the number of weights) is too high for the problem under consideration. As described in Section 2.9, the neural network learns all the details of the training patterns and has sufficient degrees of freedom to fit the noise so that the generalisation performance on the test data is very poor. For a given number of inputs I and a pre-determined number of classes K, the number of weights will vary according to the number of hidden units j. Thus the first step to overcome an over-fitting problem is to reduce the number of hidden units in the neural network model.

Over-training

Here the model order is correct; the network is given an appropriate number of hidden units but training continues for much too long (possibly because a validation set is not being used and minimisation of the error on the training set is continued well beyond the point at which the validation error would begin to rise). The result is identical: the noise on the training patterns will have been learnt, leading to a decrease in the generalisation performance on the test set.

Test examples of one class consistently wrong

This is a phenomenon often observed when the network is trained with an unbalanced database. Consider the problem of detecting tumours in X-ray mammograms. Since most women who are screened for breast cancer are healthy, there may be, say, one thousand examples of fibrous tissue regions, one thousand examples of fatty tissue regions but only ten examples of tumours in a database acquired sequentially over a period of time. If a three-class network is trained on a set of appropriate features extracted from the regions of interest, it will never learn to recognise the tumours. Minimisation of the mean squared error across the whole of the training set will optimise the fit to the two thousand examples of healthy tissue and ignore the very few pathological cases (which will be treated as outliers). This problem will not be detected unless the classification errors on the training and validation sets are specifically monitored *for each class separately* during training. When an example of a tumour occurs in the test set, the trained network will invariably classify it wrongly as one of the two healthy tissue types.

There are two possible solutions to this problem: the widely different prior probabilities of the pathologies can be taken into account (see Appendix B) or a model of normality can be constructed from examples of healthy tissue only, with tumours being subsequently detected as *novel* with respect to this representation (Tarassenko *et al.*, 1995).

Extrapolation rather than interpolation

This will arise when the network is trained on one set of conditions and then tested on a different set of conditions; for example, a network might be trained to predict the weather from data gathered during the summer and then tested during the winter. The winter data will occupy a different region of input space to the training data and so the network will be required to extrapolate, with the result that the predictions will be inaccurate. The degree of inaccuracy will depend on the distance between the input vector and the nearest training patterns (i.e. on its novelty—see Section 7.8). Prior knowledge should ensure that this type of problem does *not* arise in the first place. If, for some unexpected reason, the domain of operation changes during testing, then the network should be *re-trained* over the entire input space. An alternative, when conditions are known *not* to remain constant, is to consider on-line learning strategies (see Chapter 9) but these should only be used with a great deal of care.

8
THE CASE STUDIES

8.1 Overview of the case studies

Sleep classification

Background

The electroencephalogram, or EEG, is a record of the brain's electrical activity at a number of electrode sites on the scalp. The EEG can provide clinicians with valuable insights into the neurophysiology of sleep: for example, an examination of the EEG and related physiological signals can indicate to a trained expert whether a person lying in a darkened room is either awake, dreaming, or deeply asleep. This case study focuses on the automated classification of sleep into three types, namely, wakefulness, dreaming or rapid-eye-movement (REM) sleep, and deep sleep.

Data collection

Overnight sleep recordings were collected from nine healthy adults, and the EEGs were digitised to 8-bit accuracy at a sampling rate of 128 Hz. These EEGs were then examined by three human experts, and sections of each EEG that all three experts had identified consistently, but independently of one another, as periods during which the subject was awake, dreaming, or deeply asleep were archived. This resulted in the collection of the following amounts of consensus-scored EEG: 4920 seconds of wakefulness, 43 590 seconds of REM sleep and 42 630 seconds of deep sleep.

Pre-processing

An analysis of this digitised EEG could in theory proceed by treating each second (i.e. 128 samples) of raw EEG as a point in a 128-dimensional feature space. A huge amount of data would be required to populate adequately such a space, however, and it is known that the discriminatory information is in the frequency content of the EEG. It is therefore necessary to reduce the dimensionality of the data by some form of pre-processing which involves a frequency-domain

representation of the EEG. Whilst the fast Fourier transform (FFT) has histor-
ically been the method of popular choice, the use of an alternative technique
called autoregressive (AR) modelling carries with it a number of advantages.
For example, the dominant frequencies in a one-second section of EEG are more
accurately represented using an autoregressive model than with the FFT. Since
studies have shown that such one-second sections of EEG require the use of
a tenth-order AR model (see Pardey *et al.*, 1996a), each second of the EEG
archived above is therefore reduced to an input vector of ten AR coefficients.

Detailed explanations of autoregressive modelling techniques and sleep EEG
analysis can be found in Roberts and Tarassenko (1995) and Pardey *et al.*, (1996a
and 1996b).

Balancing the data set

The next point to consider is the need for a balanced data set. To ensure that
each class is equally represented during the training of a neural network, the data
set should contain an equal number of input vectors from each class. The size
of a balanced data set is thus determined by the class that contains the smallest
number of input vectors, which, for the three types of sleep archived above,
corresponds to the 4920 seconds of wakefulness. So by randomly selecting the
same number of vectors from the other two classes (i.e. from the 43 590 REM
sleep vectors and 42 630 deep sleep vectors), a balanced data set was created
containing 4920 vectors per class, i.e. 14 760 vectors in total. This overall data
set is then partitioned into *balanced* training, validation and test sets, each with
4920 vectors (1640 of each class). Since the frequency with which each class
occurs in all the three data sets is the same, the prior probabilities for each
class can be taken to be the same also. When this is *not* the case and there are
different probabilities between the training and test sets, Bayes' theorem must
be used to compute the true posterior probabilities from the network outputs
(see Appendix B).

Normalisation

Finally, but no less importantly, is the issue of normalisation. It is sometimes
the case that one or more of the features in a data set have small magnitudes
and dynamic ranges but little overlap between classes, while other features
with much greater overlap between the classes might have large magnitudes
and dynamic ranges. Obviously, it is the features with the least overlap that
are the most useful for classification purposes, but since RBF networks utilise
Euclidean-distance measurements, these features will be swamped by the less
useful ones. Therefore, to ensure that all of the features are given equal emphasis, a zero-mean, unit-variance normalisation procedure is usually applied to
the data. Since each 10-D vector x^p in the data set described above was stored
as a row of ten values, $x_1^p, x_2^p, \ldots, x_{10}^p$, normalisation of the 14 760 values for

each feature proceeds by first calculating the mean, μ_i, and variance, σ_i^2, for each of the ten columns in the training set according to the following formulae (see Section 7.4):

$$\mu_i = \frac{1}{P}\sum_{p=1}^{P} x_i^p \qquad \sigma_i^2 = \frac{1}{P-1}\sum_{p=1}^{P}(x_i^p - \mu_i)^2$$

where $i = 1, \ldots, 10$ and $P = 4920$ (the number of patterns in the training set). Each column is then normalised using the following linear transformation:

$$x_i^* = \frac{x_i - \mu_i}{\sigma_i}$$

This serves to equalise the magnitudes and dynamic ranges for each feature, but leaves the relative overlap between the classes unchanged.

Prediction of diabetes in Pima Indians

Background

The women of the Pima Indians, a tribe of North American Indians, are known to have a relatively high incidence of diabetes compared to Amero-Europeans. An interesting question is whether it is possible to predict whether or not a female member of the tribe is diabetic given other physiological parameters. The high incidence of diabetes among these women means that it is possible to collect data in which there is a relatively high incidence of the medical condition. This, in turn, makes it relatively simple to generate balanced training and test sets (i.e. sets in which there is an equal incidence of each possible outcome). This data set is one of the sample problems described in the first chapter of Ripley's book *Pattern Recognition and Neural Networks* (CUP, 1996).

Data collection

A study was performed in which a set of physiological parameters was measured for a group of women from the Pima tribe. The following parameters were recorded:

1. number of times pregnant;
2. plasma glucose concentration at 2 hours in an oral glucose tolerance test;
3. diastolic blood pressure (mm Hg);
4. triceps skin fold thickness (mm);
5. 2-hour serum insulin (μU/ml);
6. body mass index (weight in kg/(height in m)^2);
7. diabetes pedigree function;
8. age (years);
9. diabetic or not.

With the exception of the last piece of information, all of the measurements are numeric. The aim is to predict the final piece of information, whether or not the woman is diabetic, from the eight other pieces of information. The last piece of information is therefore the class we wish to predict using a neural network.

Pre-processing

Measurements were taken from just over 750 women. However, not all the factors were measured for all the women, so the first task was to determine how many complete records were available. Investigation revealed that just under half the records were incomplete, leaving around 380 complete records. This is a very low number of training patterns from which to generate a statistical model, so the next step was to see if it was possible to use more records, as no more data is available.

Examination of the data by eye revealed that the most frequently absent reading was the insulin measurement (number 5 in the list above). If that reading is removed, it is possible to compile a list of 532 complete records, 177 of which are records of diabetics. This is a significant increase in the size of the data set.

The removal of the insulin measurement resulted in an input space with a lower dimension and a greater number of input patterns. (Feature removal, however, should be avoided if at all possible. There is no doubt that knowledge of the insulin levels of all the women would improve the classification results. An alternative would have been to use one of the methods described in Section 6.4 for estimating the missing values.) The pruned data set consisted of 177 records for diabetic women and 355 records from non-diabetic women. A balanced data set of 176 diabetic women and 176 non-diabetic women was constructed by choosing 176 examples of the latter class at random from the 355 available examples. (176 is a much easier number to handle than 177, as will be seen later.) This data set of 352 examples is a small data set, and it is therefore necessary to use it with care. For example, it will be necessary to accumulate results during training from different random partitions of the data set (see Section 8.4).

8.2 Benchmark results

As explained at the end of Chapter 4, the two methods against which any neural network should always be evaluated are linear models (both for regression and classification) and nearest-neighbour techniques (for classification).

Both of these were applied to the sleep EEG and Pima Indians data sets. The linear classifiers are trained on the training set using either Singular Value Decomposition (SVD) for matrix inversion or the iterative Least Mean Square (LMS) algorithm. Both of these were briefly discussed in Section 2.7 in the context of training the output layer of an RBF network. For a single-layer linear classifier with an input vector $x = (x_1, x_2, \ldots, x_i, \ldots, x_n)$ and output y, the weight update rule using the LMS algorithm is simply (as in Equations (2.19) and (2.20)):

$$\Delta w_i = -\eta(y - t)x_i$$

where x_i is the value of the ith feature or parameter.

Nearest-neighbour classification is extremely simple to implement: every pattern in the test set is given the label of the nearest example (in Euclidean distance) in the training set.

Benchmark results for sleep classification

The application of both methods to sleep classification is straightforward since data is plentiful for this problem: 50% of the data is used as a training set, the rest as a test set. Ten different random splits of the data were created. For each partition, a linear classifier was trained using the LMS algorithm and its classification error on the test set recorded. The whole exercise was then repeated using SVD. The average test classification error over these twenty runs was 20.0%, with a minimum of 19.1% and a maximum of 21.3%.

Nearest-neighbour classification was also tested with the same ten partitions. The average test classification error was 18.3%, with a minimum of 17.6% and a maximum of 18.8%. As expected, there is little variation between the results for different splits of the data, both for the linear classifier and especially for the nearest-neighbour classifier. The random splitting into ten different partitions is clearly not necessary for a problem such as this one when there is no shortage of data.

Benchmark results for Pima Indians diabetes data

The relative scarcity of data for the Pima Indians data set makes the application of classification methods more difficult. As explained later on in this chapter, cross-validation techniques were used to create eleven different partitions, each with 320 training patterns and 32 test patterns. The evaluation procedure described above for the sleep EEG data set was repeated in exactly the same way, except for the fact that there were eleven 10:1 partitions rather than ten 50:50 partitions.

The most accurate linear classifier gave an error rate of 15.4%, the average error rate being 23.6% and the worst error rate being 40.6%. The corresponding figures for the nearest-neighbour classifier were a minimum error rate of 12.5%, an average of 29.2%, and a worst error rate of 46.9%. It is clear that an average figure must always be quoted when dealing with small data sets, as the 'most accurate' classifiers tend to benefit from combinations of training and test patterns that make the problem appear simpler than it is in reality. The 'benchmark figures' for this problem are therefore taken to be error rates of 23.6%

Data set	Total number of patterns used	Average test classification error	
		Linear classifier	Nearest neighbour
Sleep EEG	14 760	20.0%	18.3%
Pima Indians	352	23.6%	29.2%

Table 8.1 *Summary of linear classifier and nearest-neighbour performance.*

and of 29.2% for the linear and nearest-neighbour classifiers respectively. The overall results for both problems are summarised in Table 8.1.

8.3 Application of data visualisation to the case studies

Sleep EEG data

Introduction

Training a Kohonen feature map is divided into two phases. During phase one, the map becomes topologically ordered by coarse-tuning its cluster centres using a large neighbourhood size and high learning rate; during phase two, when the neighbourhood size has reduced to 1 and the learning rate to 0.01, the cluster centres are fine-tuned independently of one another by adaptive K-means clustering. However, prior to training a Kohonen map it is useful to gain some indication of the kind of clustering performance that can be achieved on the data set with batch K-means clustering. The reason for doing this is that the clustering performance of a Kohonen map is invariably compromised by the more important requirement of good topological ordering. This sub-optimal clustering is not actually a problem, since the motivation for using a Kohonen map in the first place is not so much to achieve the best clustering performance (for which a standard clustering algorithm would be used) but rather to provide a good visual representation of the data which might subsequently reveal the presence of any structure. Nevertheless, it clearly makes sense to use K-means clustering on the data as a performance measure by which to ascertain whether the clustering achieved with a Kohonen map is close enough to be acceptable.

It is also worth noting that for both K-means clustering and Kohonen maps, the data set does not need to be split into separate training, validation, and test sets, as it does when training an MLP. The whole data set can therefore be normalised and used directly, once the vectors in it have been properly randomised.

Benchmark results

Batch K-means clustering was performed on the 14 760 vectors in the normalised data set using $K = 100$ cluster centres. This value of K was chosen to match the number of units that were subsequently used when training a 10×10 Kohonen map. The average Mean Squared Error (MSE) obtained after five random initialisations of the K-means algorithm was 3.119, so the MSE obtained with a Kohonen map should be as close to this as possible.

Training the Kohonen map

Fifty 10×10 Kohonen maps were trained on the 14 760 vectors in the normalised data set. Each training run used between 10 and 5000 passes through the entire data set and a different initialisation of the weight vectors for the 100 units, each of which was set equal to a randomly-selected vector from the data set. Training was discontinued at the end of phase one, so that no adaptive K-means clustering was performed after the topological ordering was completed (the reason for this will become clear later). The learning rate, α, and neighbourhood size, N, were chosen to decay exponentially (although linear reduction rates would probably have been equally acceptable and are both easier and faster to calculate) according to the formulae:

$$\alpha = \alpha_0 \exp^{-t/t_\alpha} \qquad N = N_0 \exp^{-t/t_N}$$

where the values chosen for the initial learning rate, α_0, and initial neighbourhood size, N_0, were 0.9 and 200 respectively[1]. The time constants for learning rate reduction, t_α, and neighbourhood size reduction, t_N, depend on the number of passes through the data set during phase one, since at the end of this time α and N must have reduced from their initial values of 0.9 and 200 to their final values of 0.01 and 1. So when the number of passes through the data set during phase one is 100, for instance, the values for t_α and t_N would be 22.22 and 18.87 respectively, since:

$$0.01 \approx 0.9 \exp^{-100/22.22} \qquad \text{and} \qquad 1 \approx 200 \exp^{-100/18.87}$$

Results

The smallest MSE obtained from the fifty Kohonen maps was 3.592, which is about 15% higher than the average MSE obtained with batch K-means clustering. The map took 5000 passes through the data set to achieve this MSE, and yielded the distributions shown in Figure 8.1 when the 4920 vectors in each of the three classes were re-presented to it.

---

[1] In the implementation of Kohonen's learning algorithm used in this case study, the neighbourhood size is defined in terms of the squared Euclidean distance between units on the map, in which case the distance from one corner unit to the opposite corner unit is $(10\sqrt{2})^2$, i.e. 200.

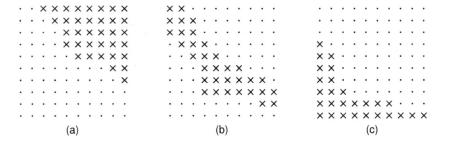

Fig. 8.1 *Distribution of 75% of the 4920 vectors for (a) wakefulness, (b) REM sleep, and (c) deep sleep.*

The crosses on each instance of the map indicate the units that are 'visited' most often by the corresponding class, i.e. the units whose associated weight vectors (or, now that the map has been trained, cluster centres) are closest to the feature vectors in that class. The reason for marking with crosses only those units that, by virtue of being visited most often, account for 75% of the feature vectors in a class, is to reveal the area(s) of the map covered by the bulk of the data for each class. Without the use of this 75% threshold, a single outlier among the 4920 vectors in a class would be enough to mark a unit as visited, even though such vectors are probably not representative of the class. Examples of this include 'drowsiness' vectors mixed in with the wakefulness data, or vectors derived from sections of EEG corrupted by movement of the scalp muscles. The choice of a 75% threshold is arbitrary, however, and there is no reason why other threshold values should not be tried.

What the distributions in Figure 8.1 reveal is that each class occupies a different region of feature space, which is encouraging when we come to design neural network classifiers in order to discriminate between the three types of EEG. If the crosses for each class had been scattered across the map, or all lying in the same region(s) of it, then we would expect the subsequent classifiers to perform poorly. Another possibility that might provide further insight into the nature of the EEG (although it is not demonstrated here) is to perform some kind of trajectory analysis, whereby the trained map is presented with feature vectors derived from continuous, one-second sections of EEG, and the time course of the EEG signal is then tracked as it moves from unit to unit around the map.

Pathologies

Experience shows that the Kohonen map algorithm seems to be fairly robust, and few problems should be encountered if one or two simple rules of thumb are observed regarding, for example, the choice of values for α_0 and N_0. A value of 0.9 is often used for α_0, although there is obviously no harm in trying a few different values to see if this affects the final mapping. Similarly, it might

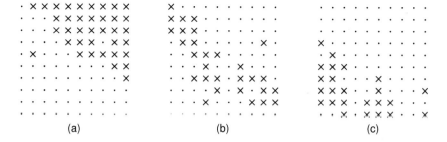

Fig. 8.2 *Fragmentation of the topological ordering in Figure 8.1 after 35 passes through the data set during phase two (adaptive K-means clustering).*

be worth trying a few different values for N_0 ranging from, say, one-half to twice the size of the map itself (50 to 200 in the current example, for which map size is defined in terms of squared Euclidean distance). The values of t_α and t_N are set by the values of α_0 and N_0 and the number of passes through the data set during phase one, while the initial values for the weight vectors are usually set equal to vectors chosen at random from the data. Although these may appear to be *ad hoc* choices, the fact remains that the algorithm works reliably and provides useful insights into data structure. Perhaps the major pitfall to be aware of occurs during phase two.

The use of adaptive K-means clustering during phase two of the Kohonen map's training needs to be handled carefully. Since the neighbourhood size, N, has reduced to 1, phase-two learning has the effect of altering the positions of the Kohonen map's prototype vectors or cluster centres in input space (and thereby improving the MSE) *without* affecting the topological ordering of the units on the 2-D map itself. It is therefore a good idea to monitor the map's performance after every iteration through the data set during phase two. Whilst a few iterations may possibly 'tighten' the distributions shown in Figure 8.1 (as well as reducing the MSE), further iterations, while continuing to reduce the MSE, will eventually cause the topological ordering established during the usually much longer period of phase-one learning to disintegrate.

To illustrate this, the Kohonen map that yielded the results shown in Figure 8.1 after 5000 passes of phase-one learning was subjected to a further 50 passes through the data set using phase-two learning. Minor disruption to the map's topological ordering was discernible after only the first pass, despite the fact that the data set itself is particularly 'well-behaved'. After 35 passes the MSE had reduced to 3.180, which is only 1.9% higher than the average MSE obtained earlier with batch K-means clustering. However, the class distributions had fragmented to the extent shown in Figure 8.2. At this point (and perhaps earlier) the inferences drawn from Figure 8.1 could no longer be made with the same confidence.

```
x  ·  ·  ·  ·  ·        x  x  x  x  x  x
x  x  ·  ·  ·  ·        ·  ·  x  x  x  ·
x  x  ·  ·  ·  ·        x  x  x  x  x  x
x  x  ·  ·  ·  ·        ·  ·  x  x  x  x
x  x  ·  x  ·  x        ·  ·  ·  ·  ·  ·
x  x  x  ·  ·  x        ·  ·  ·  ·  x  ·
      (a)                    (b)
```

Fig. 8.3 *Distribution of 75% of the 176 vectors for (a) class 0, and (b) class 1.*

Pima Indians data

Introduction

There is much less data available in the data set for the Pima Indians than for the sleep problem. It was therefore necessary to use Kohonen maps with a smaller number of units to visualise this data.

Training the Kohonen map

Fifty 6×6 Kohonen maps were trained on the 352 seven-dimensional vectors. Each run used a different number of passes through the training set and a different random initialisation. Training was discontinued when the neighbourhood size had reduced to 1, so that no adaptive K-means clustering was performed after the topological ordering was completed.

Results

The results are shown in Figure 8.3, which shows the distribution of data when the 352 vectors from the data set are re-presented to the trained map. The left-hand panel represents the distribution of 75% of the 176 vectors from non-diabetics and the right-hand half the distribution of 75% of the 176 vectors from diabetics.

The smallest MSE obtained was 1.819, which is only 3% larger than the average MSE which had been obtained in an earlier experiment using batch K-means clustering, and is therefore acceptable.

Conclusion

This section has shown that, even when the separation is less distinct than for the sleep EEG problem, the Kohonen map still shows that it ought to be possible to distinguish between the two classes (diabetics and non-diabetics) from the available physiological indicators using neural network classification techniques, despite the small number of cases available.

8.4 Application of MLPs to the case studies

Sleep classification

Data preparation

The 14 760 vectors in the data set were partitioned into balanced training, validation, and test sets, each containing 1640 vectors per class, i.e. 4920 vectors in total. It is not strictly necessary to normalise the data before using it to train MLPs (since, unlike RBFs, MLPs do not use Euclidean-distance measurements), but it is nonetheless usually advantageous to do so. This is because the time taken by the error back-propagation algorithm to train an MLP can be greatly reduced by first normalising the data, as this generally reduces the amount by which the values of the MLP's weights will have to change in order to accommodate widely different dynamic ranges in the input features. In the current example, therefore, a zero-mean, unit-variance normalisation procedure was applied to the training set, and these *same* values of mean and variance, derived from the ten columns in the training set[2] were then used to normalise the validation and test sets. The vectors in the training set were then shuffled to make sure that they are presented to the neural network in a random order (although it is not necessary to do this with the validation and test sets as these are always used in batch mode).

Training the MLP(s)

Although the number of inputs to, and outputs from, an MLP are fixed by the dimensionality of the input data and the number of output classes respectively, the 'correct' number of hidden units to use is not known in advance. As described in Chapter 7, a straightforward way of resolving this is to perform a thorough search, whereby a large number of MLPs are trained with different numbers of hidden units and different random initialisations for the weights. From all these runs, the optimal network is selected as the one which gives the minimum classification error on the validation set. To illustrate this in the context of the current example, eighty-five MLPs were trained as classifiers using the error back-propagation algorithm and 1-out-of-K output coding. Each MLP had ten inputs and three outputs ($K = 3$), but j, the number of hidden units, was varied between 4 and 20. For each of these fifteen architectures, five runs took place with different sets of (random) initial weight values. The minimum classification error rate achieved on the validation set was used to determine when to stop training each MLP, and the values of η (the learning rate) and α (the momentum coefficient) used were 0.01 and 0.6 respectively.

---

[2]As we are dealing with 10-dimensional input vectors.

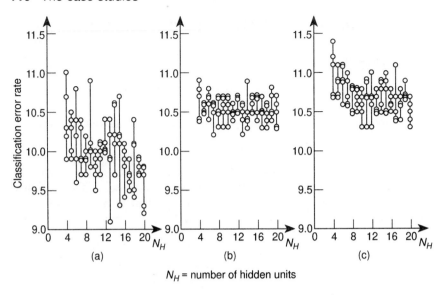

Fig. 8.4 *Percentage classification error rates on (a) the training set, (b) the validation set, and (c) the test set vs number of hidden units.*

Results

For each MLP the error back-propagation algorithm required between 22 and 215 passes through the training set to satisfy the stopping criterion described above. The results are summarised in Figure 8.4.

Figure 8.4(c) reveals that the classification error rates obtained on the test set range from 10.3% at best to 11.4% at worst. This provides a realistic indication of the level of performance that can be expected when an MLP is used to classify new data, i.e. data that it has never 'seen' before. When choosing the 'optimal' MLP, as discussed extensively in Section 7.7, the selection is based on the lowest classification error rate obtained on the *validation* set. Figure 8.4(b) reveals that a lowest value of 10.2% is achieved by two MLPs with 7 and 13 hidden units, so in the absence of a good reason to use the more complicated 10-13-3 MLP, the simpler 10-7-3 MLP is chosen. It is, of course, perfectly legitimate to select the best MLP since it is the best model in the sense that it has the lowest classification error rate on the validation set. Its generalisation performance – which is the value quoted in all cases – is then assessed *subsequently* on an independent test set. The generalisation performance for this 10-7-3 MLP (i.e. its classification error rate on the test set) is 10.6%.

A breakdown of this value into a confusion matrix provides further insight into the MLP's performance. A confusion matrix is a $K \times K$ square matrix, with as many rows and columns as there are classes. The (k, k') entry in the matrix indicates the percentage number of times the network should have given an output indicating class k but in fact gave an output indicating class k'. If the MLP made no mistakes, then there would be three figures of 100.0 along the main diagonal and all other values would be 0.0.

	W	R	S
W	84.7	14.0	1.3
R	7.8	88.0	4.2
S	0.2	4.3	95.5

The first row of the confusion matrix reveals that, after training, the MLP is able to classify correctly 84.7% of the 1640 vectors of wakefulness (W) in the test set, but misclassifies 14.0% of them as REM sleep (R) and 1.3% as deep sleep (S). Similarly, it correctly classifies 88.0% of the 1640 REM sleep vectors in the test set, but misclassifies 7.8% of them as wakefulness and 4.2% as deep sleep, and so on in row three for the 1640 deep-sleep vectors.

Finally, Figure 8.4 also demonstrates that the classification error rates obtained on the training and validation sets should not be regarded as a true indication of the expected classification performance on new data. This is because the error back-propagation algorithm works by iteratively adjusting the values of an MLP's weights in favour of an improved classification performance on the training set, and continues to do this until the classification performance on the validation set is minimised. It is hardly surprising, therefore, that the error rates in Figure 8.4(a) (training set) are significantly better than those of Figure 8.4(c): the test set is never seen by the network during training since it is only presented to the MLP once training is completed and thus assumes the role of 'new data'. Figure 8.4 is a further demonstration that performance should always be assessed on a previously unseen test set.

Pima Indians

Dealing with small data sets—the use of cross-validation

This case study introduces an additional difficulty which was not seen in the sleep analysis problem: the restricted quantity of data available to construct and evaluate the neural network model. It is precisely for this type of situation that a training methodology known as *cross-validation* is employed (see Bishop, 1995).

Cross-validation has been designed to ensure that as much information as possible is used in the training process. The approach to training so far described has been to split the available data evenly into training, validation and test sets. These data sets are then used to train different configurations and initialisations of the network. If cross-validation is used, the original data set is split up several times and the training process is performed on each split of the data set.

In practice, this allows the use of a smaller test set which enables more input vectors to be used for training. This is achieved as follows:

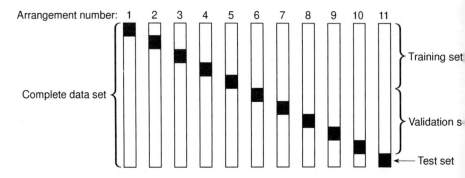

Fig. 8.5 *The 11 arrangements of the training data used: a different eleventh (shaded) is used for each of the 11 trials.*

- The total data set is split up into S subsets, each of equal size.
- For each subset, that subset is chosen to be the test set and the other $S-1$ subsets are combined to form the training and validation sets.

For this problem, the total number of available training patterns is limited by the number of patients with diabetes (177). The number 177 is only divisible by 3 and 59, so to perform cross-validation with 177 patterns would require that each subset contains either 3 or 59 patterns. The latter case (3 subsets of 59 patterns) is too few subsets, the former (59 subsets of 3 patterns) has too few patterns in each subset. However, 176 is divisible by 11, giving 11 subsets of 16 patterns. The data set was therefore reduced to 176 patterns from women with diabetes and the same number from women without diabetes. For each of the 11 partitions, the remaining $S-1$ subsets were arranged to give 80 training patterns and 80 validation patterns from each class (i.e. 320 patterns in all), the test set consisting of the remaining 32 patterns (16 from each class). This is shown diagrammatically in Figure 8.5. It should be clear from the figure that the use of cross-validation techniques removes any dependence on which patterns are chosen as the test set. By the time the results are averaged across all 11 partitions, each of the 352 patterns will have appeared as a test pattern once.

Training the MLP

With this problem, the MLP has a single output which is an estimate of the posterior probability that the woman is diabetic given the seven physiological indicators used as inputs. With an MLP, it is not necessary to apply a zero-mean, unit-variance transform to the input data but nevertheless such a transformation is helpful in order to compensate for variations in dynamic range, as explained in Section 7.4.

Results

For each partition of the data, several configurations and initialisations of MLP were trained. Initial experiments showed that the optimal number of hidden units was six (with $\eta = 0.1$ and $\alpha = 0.6$). As before, the best MLPs must be chosen on the basis of lowest classification error on the validation set. This time however, the situation is complicated by the fact that there are 11 partitions. We must therefore find an optimal MLP *for each partition* and evaluate its generalisation performance on the test set corresponding to that partition. Averaging these results across all 11 partitions will give the best estimate of generalisation performance, as every pattern will have been used once as a test pattern. As pointed out in the previous chapter, the recommended mode of operation from then on is to use a committee of all 11 networks.

The more complicated procedure suggested above can be implemented by slightly modifying the method described in Section 7.7. The pseudo-code is shown below:

```
for (loop = 1; loop <= 10; loop++)
{
        initial weight set[loop] = random;
        for (p = 1; p <= 11; p++)
        {
            weight set = initial weight set[loop];
            train MLP by updating weight set;
            stop when (eval)min has been reached;
            if (eval)min < (eval)opt[p]
            {
                (eval)opt[p] = (eval)min;
                optimal weight set[p] = weight set;
            }
        }
}
for (p = 1; p <= 11; p++)
evaluate test error[p] on that partition using optimal weight set[p];
```

With the 10 different random initialisations (corresponding to each value of 'loop') and the 11 different partitions, there are 110 different MLPs to train and test. The optimal network is identified for each partition and the corresponding weight set is saved. At the end of this procedure, the test error is evaluated on each partition using the appropriate weight set. The average training, validation and test errors were found to be 18.6%, 21.1% and 22.7% respectively.

The above procedure may appear very convoluted but such a systematic approach is required in order to obtain a *fair* estimate of the best generalisation performance which can be achieved. The misleading nature of results obtained

	Average error for 10 best MLPs		
	Training set	Validation set	Test set
7-6-1 MLP	18.6%	21.1%	22.7%
7-100-1 MLP	18.1%	20.1%	23.9%

Table 8.2 *The effect of using too many hidden units.*

when optimising performance on the test set is well illustrated on this data set: when the above procedure was repeated but this time the ten best networks were chosen on the basis of the lowest *test* error, regardless of partition, the average test error rate was found to be 12.2%! *If new test data became available, however, there is no doubt that networks trained using this erroneous procedure would perform considerably worse since they are highly tuned to the idiosyncracies of their very small test sets.*

Pathologies

Having established what can be achieved through the careful use of the MLP training procedure, we will now demonstrate some common pitfalls.

Too many hidden units

If too many hidden units are used, it is likely that the network will begin to act like an associative memory, storing the individual training points and their desired outputs rather than learning the underlying function. For example, a 100 hidden unit MLP was trained using the cross-validation procedure described above on 10 different initialisations of the network. The best 10 MLPs were selected (again on the basis of the lowest classification error on the validation set) and the results are given in Table 8.2. The results in the table demonstrate that for similar errors in the validation set, the error on the training set is lower for the MLPs with 100 hidden units but the error on the test set is higher. This not only demonstrates the need for keeping the number of hidden units sufficiently low but also reinforces the point that performance should always be evaluated on an independent test set.

Unbalanced training set

An unbalanced training set is one in which one class of output is more represented than another. The use of such training sets can result in poor generalisation performance (unless the different *a priori* probabilities are taken into account—see Appendix B). To demonstrate this, two trial experiments were set up. There is no other diabetic data available and so one way to introduce an imbalance would be to add some of the unused non-diabetic data. With the available data set, however, this would only lead to a 2:1 imbalance. A more substantial imbalance was artificially set up by *removing* data: the second experiment described below was carried out with subsets containing 16 examples of non-diabetics, as before, but only 4 diabetics. In order to have the same amount of training data to allow for a fair comparison, a prior experiment was first performed with balanced subsets also containing 20 examples (10 non-diabetics, 10 diabetics). The two experiments are summarised below:

1. The cross-validation scheme described above was employed as before but each subset was only given 10 examples of each class, whilst the test set retained 16 examples of each class: 11 different network initialisations were used, giving, as before, 110 trained networks.
2. The cross-validation scheme was used but each subset now had only 4 diabetics as compared with 16 non-diabetics. This means that there are the same number of patterns in the training set as in Experiment 1, but now with a different distribution between the two classes. The test set again had 16 examples of each class and 110 different networks were trained separately.

From each set of 110 networks, the best 10 were chosen on the basis of minimum validation error and their test errors were then averaged to give the results summarised in Table 8.3. It is clear from the table that the networks trained using the unbalanced training sets have performed far worse than the networks trained using a balanced training set.

Poor choice of learning rate

The choice of learning rate can have a significant effect on the performance of an MLP. As before, the cross-validation procedure was applied to 10 different initialisations of the network for each of 6 learning rates: 0.0001, 0.001, 0.01, 0.1, 1.0 and 10.0. Both the average error subsequently evaluated on the test set for the best ten networks and the number of epochs necessary to achieve the minimum error on the validation set are given in Table 8.4. The algorithm trained the network for a further 100 passes through the data set (epochs) after the optimal result was achieved to ensure that no benefit could be obtained from further training.

From Table 8.4, it can be seen that, if the learning rate is too small, it takes a much larger number of epochs to train an MLP because each update of the network weights is proportional to the learning rate (see Equations (2.8) and (2.10) in Chapter 2). When the learning rate is too high, sub-optimal networks are obtained, but faster. Consequently, a well-chosen learning rate will move the weights towards their optimal values (for that training and validation set) in reasonable time. Too large a learning rate will result in updates that move the weights too far in the direction 'towards' these optimal values but beyond the optimal solution.

Number of patterns in each subset		Error on (balanced) test set
Non-diabetic	Diabetic	
10	10	21.3%
16	4	33.5%

Table 8.3 *The effect of using unbalanced training sets.*

Learning rate	Average error on test set	Average number of passes required
0.0001	22.7%	7576
0.001	22.7%	1814
0.01	22.7%	248
0.1	22.7%	35
1.0	25.6%	14
10.0	24.7%	51

Table 8.4 *The effect of using different learning rates.*

8.5   Application of RBF networks to the case studies

Sleep classification

Data preparation

As discussed in Chapter 2, there is no need for a validation set with an RBF network. The free parameters in the first layer (the centre positions and widths) are set using *unsupervised* learning. The weights of the second layer are found using a linear optimisation procedure, either by matrix inversion (using the SVD algorithm) or iteratively with the LMS algorithm. When using the latter procedure, training is stopped when no further reduction of Mean Squared Error (MSE) can be achieved with additional iterations (the plot of the MSE with iteration number has become flat). In this part of the case study, 2400 vectors from each of the three classes were used to generate balanced training and test sets, each with a total of 7200 vectors.

Training the first layer

As already seen in Chapter 2, the K-means algorithm is the standard method for the first (unsupervised) phase of training an RBF network. There are two versions of the K-means algorithm: batch and adaptive. The batch version is far superior: it has both a stopping criterion (i.e. there is a definite point at which one can say that no further reduction of the MSE will be achieved by further iterations) and does not require a 'learning coefficient' to be set. For this work, therefore, the batch K-means algorithm was used for determining the centre positions.

Once the positions of the centres μ_j had been obtained, the widths σ_j were set to be the average distance between the centres μ_j and the training patterns which belong to that cluster:

$$\sigma_j^2 = \frac{1}{p_j} \sum_{x \in C_j} (x - \mu_j)^T (x - \mu_j)$$

where C_j is the set of training patterns grouped with centre μ_j and p_j is the number of patterns in C_j (see Equation (2.18) in Chapter 2).

Training the second layer

The set of centres obtained at the end of the first phase of learning was then used as the hidden units of a 10-j-3 RBF network, where j is the number of centres. The output layer weights were calculated using either the LMS algorithm or matrix inversion using SVD. The two methods usually give almost identical results (since they are trying to arrive at the same global minimum).

Results

An exhaustive search was carried out to determine the optimal number of centres, ten different random partitions of the overall data set into equal numbers of training and test patterns being generated for each value of j. The average error rate for the ten best RBFs (i.e. those with the minimum training error in this case, the 'global' optimum for the given centre positions and widths) was 11.6%. The number of centres varied from 2 to 150, the results being shown in Figure 8.6. Again the results obtained using SVD and LMS are broadly similar.

Pima Indians

Data partitioning

The data was partitioned using the same cross-validation procedure as for MLP training, except that there is no need for a validation set; thus, each of the 11 different partitions had 320 training patterns (160 from each class) and 32 test patterns.

Input data normalisation and network initialisation

As previously discussed, the data was normalised so that, after normalisation, it had a mean of 0.0 and a variance of 1.0. Patterns from the training database were selected at random in order to create the initial set of centres.

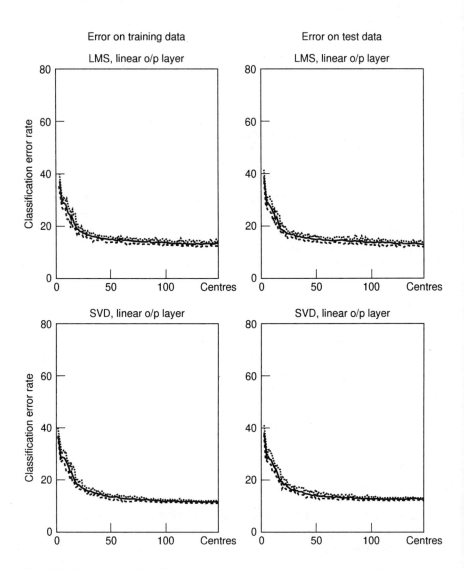

Fig. 8.6 *Percentage classification error rates on the training set and on the test set vs number of centres (from 2 to 150).*

Data set	No. of patterns	Linear classifier	Nearest neighbour	MLP	RBF
Sleep EEG	14 760	20.0%	18.3%	10.6%	11.6%
Pima Indians	352	23.6%	29.2%	22.7%	26.3%

Table 8.5 *Average test classification errors – summary of results.*

Results

Various network configurations were tried with an upper limit of 150 hidden units. It is sensible to set an upper limit between $P/10$ and $P/2$ (where, as before, P is the number of training patterns) to ensure that the network does not overfit. The trained network should act as an approximator of the relationship between the input and output data sets, not as a pseudo-memory of the training set.

For each combination of network size (between 2 and 150 hidden units), the minimum error rate was identified for each partition. The best RBF network's performance on the training set (averaged across all partitions) was obtained from a network with 112 hidden units. The generalisation performance of this network, estimated by averaging the test error rate across all 11 partitions, was found to be 26.3%.

8.6 Conclusions

The results summarised in Table 8.5 in this chapter show clearly the value of a non-linear mapping on the sleep classification problem. The error rate is almost halved in going from a linear classifier to an MLP, a very significant improvement. The performance of the RBF network on the same data set is not far behind (see the end of the previous chapter for a discussion of the advantages of the RBF network with respect to the MLP).

The Pima Indians data set is a publicly available data set which is often used as a benchmark problem for assessing the performance of neural classifiers. The results given in Table 8.5 show clearly, however, that any benchmarking should be done against *linear* and nearest-neighbour techniques in the first instance. As has been demonstrated on similar problems (Ripley *et al.*, 1997), linear techniques often do very well on problems of medical prognosis. Here the MLP is only seen to give a marginal improvement. With such a small database, there are not enough patterns to provide adequate coverage of input space and it is not surprising that the RBF network does not perform well.

All of these issues, together with the need to optimise performance *before* considering the test data, should remain uppermost in the minds of the designers throughout the design process.

9
MORE ADVANCED TOPICS

9.1 Introduction

The material covered from Chapter 2 to Chapter 8 is more than sufficient for applying neural network techniques successfully to real-world problems. In this chapter, a brief overview is given of more recent developments in the field of neural computing. For some applications, these more advanced topics may give an advantage to the experienced practitioner. This chapter is not intended to be an exhaustive description of advanced techniques, merely a pointer to them. Sufficient references to published work have been included to allow the interested reader to investigate the techniques further and in greater depth.

9.2 Data visualisation

Sammon's mapping

The mapping of a data set consisting of n-dimensional vectors $x^1, \ldots, x^P$ onto a 2-dimensional space for visualisation purposes is known in the pattern recognition literature as *multi-dimensional scaling*. It is not possible to preserve the structure of the data exactly when mapping onto a lower-dimensional space (even when mapping from 3-D to 2-D) and so dimensionality-reduction algorithms are based on a variety of criteria. With Kohonen's feature map, *topology* is preserved so that neighbouring units in the feature map correspond to prototype vectors which are close to each other in the original high-dimensional space. With Sammon's mapping (Sammon, 1969), we look for a configuration of image points $y^1, \ldots, y^P$, in the 2-D visualisation space, for which the $P(P-1)/2$ distances d_{ij} between image points are as close as possible to the corresponding original distances δ_{ij}, where δ_{ij} is the Euclidean distance between x^i and x^j in the original n-dimensional input space. As already stated, it is not possible to find a configuration for which $d_{ij} = \delta_{ij}$ and so we need a criterion for assessing the suitability of a configuration with respect to the others. Sammon's mapping uses the following sum-of-squared error criterion:

$$E_S^2 = \frac{1}{\sum_{i<j} \delta_{ij}} \sum_{i<j} \frac{(d_{ij} - \delta_{ij})^2}{\delta_{ij}}$$

An optimal configuration is then obtained through gradient descent starting with some initial configuration and changing the y^is in the direction of greatest rate of decrease in the criterion function.

One advantage of the Sammon map is that it does not have the constraint of a rectangular grid: the image points are displayed in the 2-D space according to their relative Euclidean distance in this space thereby giving a better indication of the true proximity of clusters. Furthermore, there is an error function which is minimised and this allows comparison between the different local minima which are obtained as a result of different random initialisations. One minor disadvantage of Sammon's mapping is that it requires a pre-clustering phase (using the K-means algorithm) to reduce the value of P if the database contains large numbers of patterns since there are $P^2/2$ distances to be adjusted in the visualisation space. Input patterns are then mapped onto the nearest cluster centre in the Sammon map for visualisation purposes.

The application of the Sammon map to the sleep EEG data of Chapter 8 is described in Tarassenko and Roberts (1994). The Sammon map is not, strictly speaking, a neural network technique. However, recent work (Tipping and Lowe, 1997) has endowed it with interpolation properties in the 2-D visualisation space and this has been achieved by using an RBF network to learn the mapping from the high-dimensional input space to the 2-D visualisation space.

Generative Topographic Mappings

The Generative Topographic Mapping (GTM) is a probabilistic alternative to Kohonen's feature map (Bishop *et al.*, 1996 and 1997). Kohonen's algorithm has had many successful applications, but it also has a number of drawbacks: there is no error function to be minimised, there is no proof of convergence, and the learning rate as well as the neighbourhood size reduction rate (which control the topographic ordering) are chosen by trial and error.

The aim of both Kohonen's feature map and Sammon's mapping is to find a projection from n-dimensional space onto a 2-D visualisation space. The GTM algorithm is a *generative* model which defines a mapping from the visualisation or *latent* space *onto* the n-dimensional space. For the purposes of data visualisation, the mapping is then inverted using Bayes' theorem.

With GTM, a function $f(y; W)$ maps each point y in the 2-D latent space into corresponding points $x(y; W)$ in data space. The latent-variable space is mapped into a 2-dimensional non-Euclidean manifold embedded within the n-dimensional data space (i.e. the 2-D visualisation space is stretched and distorted when mapped onto data space). The unconditional probability distribution in latent space, $p(y)$, by analogy with the Kohonen feature map, is chosen to be a sum of delta functions centred on the nodes of a regular grid in latent space. The function $f(y; W)$ is given by a generalised linear network of the form:

$$f(y; W) = W\phi(y)$$

where the elements of $\phi(y)$ consist of fixed basis functions (radially symmetric Gaussians as in an RBF network). As a result of using this mapping f together with the sum of delta functions distribution for $p(y)$, each node in latent space becomes a centre in a (constrained) Gaussian mixture model in data space. The free parameters of the mixture model are determined using the Expectation-Maximisation (EM) algorithm (Dempster *et al.*, 1977). Each data point x in the original n-dimensional space induces a posterior distribution in y-space. For data visualisation purposes, x is projected to a unique point in y-space, usually the mean of the posterior distribution.

The main advantage of GTM over Kohonen's feature map is that it defines an explicit probability density function in data space. Furthermore, the neighbourhood-preserving nature of the mapping is a direct consequence of the choice of a smooth, continuous function $f(y; W)$ (Bishop *et al.*, 1996a).

9.3   Multi-layer perceptrons

Conjugate gradients

Gradient descent, even with the inclusion of a momentum term, is not necessarily a very efficient algorithm for minimising the sum-of-squared error function E at the output of an MLP. This probably does not matter too much for small to medium size problems for which good local minima of the error function can be reached in reasonable time, and indeed this was the approach adopted for all of the systematic studies carried out in Chapter 8.

The neural computing literature is full of papers describing algorithms which purport to improve the performance of basic gradient descent. However, as with the assessment of special-purpose hardware discussed in Chapter 5, it is almost impossible to determine the true worth of these (mostly *ad hoc*) modifications to simple gradient descent, as they are invariably tested on just one or two benchmark problems of the authors' choice.

The optimisation algorithm should arrive at a minimum of the error function E in the W-dimensional weight space in as few steps as possible. With basic gradient descent, the direction of each step is given by the local negative gradient of the error function and the step size is fixed by the value of η, the learning rate parameter. It turns out that moving along a search direction given by the local negative gradient vector is not the optimal strategy; rather it is better to construct a sequence of successive search directions such that each is *conjugate* to all previous directions (see Bishop, 1995, page 276, for a detailed explanation).

This is the basis of *conjugate gradient* optimisation algorithms (Press *et al.*, 1992; Bishop, 1995) which also allow the step length in each search direction to be determined automatically. Finally, a modification known as the *scaled conjugate gradient* algorithm has been introduced by Møller (1993) to make the algorithm more computationally efficient by minimising the number of times the error function has to be evaluated.

Regularisation techniques

We saw in Section 2.9 that the problem of defining the architecture of an MLP is effectively one of choosing the correct number of hidden units. Too many hidden units and over-fitting to the noise on the training data will occur. The method advocated to overcome this problem was the use of a validation set during training. The optimal network architecture was determined to be the one which gave the lowest classification error on the validation set. This strategy is sometimes known as *early stopping* since training stops before the error is minimised on the training set. Its use was demonstrated extensively in the course of the case studies of Chapter 8.

An alternative to early stopping is to construct networks with 'generous' numbers of hidden units but to use *regularisation techniques* to generate a smooth mapping which does *not* fit the noise on the training data. Regularisation involves adding a penalty term Ω to the squared error function E to give a new error function E' such that

$$E' = E + \mu\Omega$$

The degree of regularisation is controlled by the multiplicative constant μ. As usual, training proceeds by minimising the error function, E' in this case, which means that $\partial\Omega/\partial w$ should be reasonably straightforward to compute. The most popular form of regulariser is *weight decay* (Hinton, 1987; Bishop, 1995) whereby Ω is simply the sum of the squares of all the weights in the network:

$$\Omega = \frac{1}{2}\sum_i w_i^2$$

The weight update equation then becomes:

$$\Delta w_i = -\eta\frac{\partial E}{\partial w_i} - \eta\mu w_i$$

Weight decay encourages the function $f(x; W)$ fitted to be smooth (Ripley *et al.*, 1997). With unrestricted weight magnitudes, it is simple to fit a network which maps close input values to opposite ends of the range of $\sum w_i x_i$ values spanned by the sigmoid activation function. For example, in a two-layer MLP with one input and two hidden units, the output y_1 of the first hidden unit will be $1/(1 + \exp-(w_0 + w_1 x))$, where x is the input, w_0 is the bias weight for the first hidden unit and w_1 is the weight from the input to that unit. To map inputs of 0.1 and 0.2, say, to the extremes of the sigmoid function (taken to be ± 4.0 — see Section 7.4), we need:

$$w_0 + 0.1 w_1 = -4.0$$
$$w_0 + 0.2 w_1 = +4.0$$

which implies $w_1 = 80$ and $w_0 - -12$. To make the split between 0.1 and 0.11, the weights would have to be 800 and -84, respectively. If the other hidden unit splits in the reverse direction at 0.09, say, then a spike will be produced. Penalising large weights will make such behaviour less likely and produces a smoother mapping.

9.4 On-line learning

With true on-line learning, the neural network weights are updated each time a new input pattern becomes available, *after which time this pattern is never seen again*. This differs from sequential learning, as defined in Section 7.7 and used throughout the case studies, for which the weights are similarly updated after the presentation of each pattern but the same pattern is seen many times (once per epoch) during the training procedure. On-line learning is applied to problem domains in which batch and recursive training processes are not viable options (Lowe and McLachlan, 1995). Such problems may be found in adaptive control, adaptive signal processing or time-series forecasting.

The aim therefore is to model a non-stationary environment using an adaptive non-linear model. On-line learning allows the model to be adapted continuously as the statistics of the time-varying data generator evolve with time. The non-linear model could be an MLP or an RBF network but the characteristics of the latter lend themselves much more readily to on-line learning. The early work by Platt (1991) is a modification of an RBF network called the Resource Allocating Network, in which the number of Gaussian basis functions is increased dynamically as the input patterns are presented sequentially and then discarded. When a pattern is presented to the Resource Allocating Network, a new basis function is added to the network if the pattern is sufficiently novel with respect to previously seen data or the network parameters in *both* layers are updated using gradient descent (see Section 2.17 on the training of an RBF network). The test for novelty depends on two criteria:

1. Is the Euclidean distance between the input pattern and the nearest existing centre greater than a threshold $\delta(\tau)$?
2. Is the mean squared error at the output greater than a desired accuracy ϵ?

A new centre is allocated whenever *both* of the novelty criteria are satisfied, while errors less than ϵ are minimised using gradient descent (adjustment of second-layer weights w_{jk} and centre positions μ_j). The distance $\delta(\tau)$ represents the scale of resolution being fitted by the network; it starts from an initial value δ_{max} and is reduced exponentially with a decay rate τ until it reaches δ_{min}. The main drawback with the algorithm, however, is the number of parameters which have to be set *a priori* by the user and which may require careful tuning for optimal performance: ϵ, δ_{max}, δ_{min}, τ, κ, a width-setting parameter, and α, the learning rate for updating the weights in the second layer.

An improvement to the Resource Allocating Network was developed by Kadirkamanathan and Niranjan (1993), in which parameters were optimised within an Extended Kalman Filter framework and an improved description of model complexity was provided. More recently, Lowe and McLachlan (1995) have extended this approach from a Bayesian perspective but there are still outstanding issues to be resolved. On-line learning is a complex problem in which convergence to a stable model has to be traded off against the ability to adapt to novel data and consequently much work remains to be done in this area.

9.5   Introduction to Netlab

As mentioned in Chapter 5, public-domain software is available for neural computing application development and research. An example of such software is the Netlab library, based on the approach and techniques described in *Neural Networks for Pattern Recognition* (Bishop, 1995). The library includes software implementations of a wide range of data analysis techniques, many of which are not widely available, and are rarely included in standard neural network simulation packages.

The Netlab software is freely available from the Aston University World Wide Web site (http://www.ncrg.aston.ac.uk/). The algorithms include:

- Gaussian mixture model with EM training algorithm;
- linear regression and generalised linear models;
- multi-layer perceptron (MLP) with linear, logistic and softmax outputs and appropriate error functions;
- radial basis function (RBF) networks with both Gaussian and non-local basis functions;
- a range of optimisers, including quasi-Newton methods, conjugate gradients and scaled conjugate gradients.
- MLP with Gaussian mixture outputs (mixture density networks);
- evidence framework for Bayesian inference;
- Automatic Relevance Determination for input selection;
- Gaussian Processes;
- K-means clustering;
- K-nearest neighbour classifier;
- Generative Topographic Map (together with Kohonen Feature Map and Factor Analysis).

Netlab is implemented as a set of functions written in the Matlab® language and requires the Matlab environment to run. (Matlab is an extendible technical computing environment offering powerful numeric computation and visualisation tools.) Netlab uses only core Matlab functions, so is not dependent on any of the optional toolboxes. In particular, Netlab is distinct from, and much more powerful than, the Matlab Neural Networks Toolbox, and the optimisation functions are compatible with the Matlab Optimisation Toolbox, but do not use any functions in that toolbox. The integration with Matlab means that powerful facilities are available to pre-process the data, graph important variables, and visualise results. In addition, Matlab programs that use Netlab are portable across all main platforms and operating systems (including UNIX®, Microsoft Windows® and Apple Macintosh® environments).

Documentation is provided in two forms: brief information is provided via the Matlab help system, while a full on-line reference manual is supplied in HTML, which can be read with any suitable browser (such as Netscape®). Netlab is provided with demonstration programs and data sets to illustrate its use on a variety of problems.

Appendix A
THE ERROR BACK-PROPAGATION ALGORITHM FOR WEIGHT UPDATES IN AN MLP

For pattern p, we can re-write Equation (2.6) in Section 2.8 as follows:

$$E = \frac{1}{2}\sum_k (y_k - t_k)^2 = \frac{1}{2}\sum_k \left(g(\sum_j w_{jk}y_j) - t_k\right)^2 \qquad \text{(A.1)}$$

For a w_{jk} weight, the minimization of E by gradient descent can be expressed as

$$\Delta w_{jk} = -\eta\frac{\partial E}{\partial w_{jk}} \qquad \text{(A.2)}$$

We can expand $\partial E/\partial w_{jk}$ using the chain rule:

$$\frac{\partial E}{\partial w_{jk}} = \frac{\partial E}{\partial a_k}\frac{\partial a_k}{\partial w_{jk}} \qquad \text{where } a_k = \sum_j w_{jk}y_j$$

The first of the two terms on the right-hand side is expanded as follows:

$$\frac{\partial E}{\partial a_k} = \frac{\partial E}{\partial y_k}\frac{dy_k}{da_k}$$

If we now work out each of these in turn

$$\frac{\partial E}{\partial y_k} = y_k - t_k \qquad \text{from Equation (A.1)}$$

$$\frac{dy_k}{da_k} = \frac{dg}{da_k} = \frac{d}{da_k}\left(\frac{1}{1+e^{-a_k}}\right) = \frac{e^{-a_k}}{(1+e^{-a_k})^2} = y_k(1-y_k)$$

and combine these results with the fact that $\partial a_k/\partial w_{jk} = y_j$, we can now substitute all of this into Equation (A.2) to give:

$$\Delta w_{jk} = -\eta\frac{\partial E}{\partial w_{jk}} = -\eta\delta_k y_j$$

$$\text{where } \delta_k = \frac{\partial E}{\partial a_k} = (y_k - t_k)y_k(1-y_k)$$

The extension of the above to the w_{ij} weights from the input to the hidden units only requires the further application of the chain rule since the output error is a continuous differentiable function of these weights also, as shown in Equation (2.7) in Section 2.8.

$$\text{Thus } \Delta w_{ij} = -\eta \frac{\partial E}{\partial w_{ij}}$$

$$\text{with } \frac{\partial E}{\partial w_{ij}} = \frac{\partial E}{\partial a_j} \frac{\partial a_j}{\partial w_{ij}} \qquad \text{where } a_j = \sum_i w_{ij} y_i$$

Note that, for consistency of notation, y_i represents the ith input feature here (rather than x_i, as before). Expanding $\partial E/\partial a_j$ as before, we obtain

$$\frac{\partial E}{\partial a_j} = \frac{\partial E}{\partial y_j} \frac{dy_j}{da_j} = \frac{\partial E}{\partial y_j} y_j(1-y_j)$$

We must now find a means of evaluating $\partial E/\partial y_j$ because we cannot work it out directly (as with $\partial E/\partial y_k$). We use the fact that we have just computed $\delta_k = \partial E/\partial a_k$ in order to obtain Δw_{jk}.

$$\text{Thus } \frac{\partial E}{\partial y_j} = \frac{\partial E}{\partial a_k} \frac{\partial a_k}{\partial y_j} = \sum_k \delta_k w_{jk}$$

summing over k since each of the j hidden units is connected to all of the k output units. The update equation for the input-to-hidden weights therefore is

$$\Delta w_{ij} = -\eta \frac{\partial E}{\partial w_{ij}} = -\eta \delta_j y_i$$

$$\text{where } \delta_j = \frac{\partial E}{\partial a_j} = \sum_k \delta_k w_{jk} y_j(1-y_j)$$

Appendix B
USE OF BAYES' THEOREM TO COMPENSATE FOR DIFFERENT PRIOR PROBABILITIES

Consider, by way of an illustration, an image analysis problem in which two classes of objects have to be recognised. It is known, from data gathered over several years, that, on average, 5% of the objects to be found in these images belong to class A, 95% to class B. Thus the prior probabilities for the two classes are given by:

$$P(C_A) = 0.05 \qquad P(C_B) = 1.0 - P(C_A) = 0.95$$

A neural network is to be trained to recognise the two types of objects from features extracted from the images in the database. The database contains 1000 examples of class A and 19 000 of class B. If the neural network was trained using this database, it would learn an input–output mapping which fitted the features from class B very well but mostly ignored those from class A, as there are 19 times as many examples of class B as there are of class A. Consequently, objects from the latter class could not be reliably recognised in test data.

The solution to this is firstly to construct a *balanced* database by selecting, at random, 1000 examples from class B and combining them with the 1000 examples from class A. These 2000 examples can then be divided into training, validation and test sets, each of which will have equal numbers of examples from each class. In effect, we have skewed the prior probabilities (as in the case studies) so that

$$P'(C_A) = P'(C_B) = 0.5$$

The generalisation performance can again be evaluated on the test set for which the prior probabilities are the same as for the training and validation sets.

The neural network system is now to be used 'live' to recognise objects in images as these are being generated. An object from class B will again be 19 times more frequent than one from class A but the network was trained on a *balanced* database with equal priors. The final part of the solution involves a simple transformation, derived from Bayes' theorem (see Section 2.10), which is applied to the output of the neural network. Two quantities are computed:

$$A = \frac{\text{(Network output)} \cdot \text{(Actual Class A probability)}}{\text{(Fraction of Class A in training set)}}$$

$$B = \frac{(1.0 - \text{Network output}) \cdot (1.0 - \text{Class A probability})}{(1.0 - \text{Fraction of Class A in training set})}$$

If y is the network output, then we can write:

$$A = \frac{y \cdot P(C_A)}{P'(C_A)}$$

$$B = \frac{(1.0 - y) \cdot (1.0 - P(C_A))}{(1.0 - P'(C_A))}$$

The posterior probability of Class A is then given by:

$$P(C_A \mid x) = \frac{A}{(A + B)}$$

This transformation can make a significant difference. If, for the object recognition problem described above, the output y from the neural network trained on the balanced database is 0.8, then the posterior probability $P(C_A \mid x)$ given by this formula is 0.174 since:

$$A = \frac{0.8 \times 0.05}{0.5} = 0.08 \qquad B = \frac{0.2 \times 0.95}{0.5} = 0.38$$

$$P(C_A \mid x) = \frac{0.08}{0.46} = 0.174$$

Thus, instead of the network predicting class A with confidence (since 0.8 is well above a threshold of 0.5), the corrected prediction is in fact very clearly in favour of class B. It can be shown easily that a network output of at least 0.95 is required for the corrected prediction to be for class A.

There is one *caveat* about the use of this formula. It should not be used when the difference in prior probabilities is very large. For example, if $P(C_A)$ is only 0.001, it can be shown that the network output needs to be at least 0.999 for class A to be predicted after the correction has been applied. We know that network outputs will have errors associated with them (see Section 7.8) and it is not possible to know y to such an accuracy. Hence, in such cases, the use of this formula is to be avoided and novelty detection methods[1] should be used instead (Bishop, 1994; Tarassenko *et al.*, 1995).

---

[1] Where examples of class A are considered too novel with respect to a model of normality built from examples of class B only.

References

Baum EB and Haussler D (1989). What size net gives valid generalisation? *Neural Computation*, **1**, 151–160.

Bishop CM (1994). Novelty detection and neural network validation. *IEE Proceedings, Vision, Image & Signal Processing*, **141**, 217–222.

Bishop CM (1995). *Neural Networks for Pattern Recognition*. Oxford University Press, Oxford.

Bishop CM, Svensen M and Williams CKI. (1996). GTM: a principled alternative to the self-organizing map. *Proc. 1996 Int. Conf. on Artificial Neural Networks, ICANN96*, 165–170, Bochum, Germany, Springer-Verlag.

Bishop CM, Svensen M and Williams CKI (1997). GTM: the generative topographic mapping. *Neural Computation*, in press.

Boon ME and Kok LP (1995). Classification of cells in cervical smears. In: *Applications of Neural Networks*, Murray AF, ed., 113–131, Kluwer.

Corbett-Clark T and Tarassenko L (1997). A principled framework and technique for rule extraction from multi-layer perceptrons. *Proc. 5th IEE Int. Conf. on Artificial Neural Networks*, Cambridge, 233–238.

Cybenko G (1989). Approximation by superpositions of a sigmoidal function. *Math. Control, Signals & Systems*, **2**, 304–314.

DeMers D and Cottrell G (1993). Non-linear dimensionality reduction. In: *Advances in Neural Information Processing Systems*, **5**, Hanson SJ *et al.*, eds, MIT Press, Cambridge, Massachusetts, 580–587.

Dempster AP, Laird NM and Rubin DB (1977). Maximum likelihood from incomplete data via the EM algorithm. *J. Roy. Statist. Soc.* B **39**, 1–38.

Hassoun MH (1995). *Fundamentals of Artificial Neural Networks*. MIT Press, Cambridge, Massachusetts.

Hertz J, Krogh A and Palmer RG (1991). *Introduction to the Theory of Neural Computation*. Addison-Wesley, California.

Heskes T (1997). Practical confidence and prediction intervals. In: *Advances in Neural Information Processing Systems*, **9**, Mozer MC *et al.*, eds, MIT Press, Cambridge, Massachusetts, 176–182.

Hinton GE (1987). Connectionist learning procedures. *Artificial Intelligence*, **40**, 185–234.

Hopfield JJ (1982). Neural networks and physical systems with emergent collective computational abilities. *Proc. Nat. Acad. Sci. USA*, **79**, 2554–2558.

Hopfield JJ (1984). Neurons with graded response have collective computational properties like those of two-state neurons. *Proc. Nat. Acad. Sci. USA*, **81**, 3088–3092.

Hornik K, Stinchcombe M and White H (1989). Multilayer feedforward networks are universal approximators. *Neural Networks*, **2**, 359–366.

Hush DR and Horne BG (1993). Progress in supervised neural networks: What's new since Lippmann? *IEEE Signal Processing Magazine*, August issue, 8–39.

James M (1985). *Classification Algorithms*. Collins, London.

James H (1997). Editorial. *Neural Computing and Applications*, **5**, 129–130.

Kadirkamanathan V and Niranjan M (1993). A function estimation approach to sequential learning with neural networks. *Neural Computation*, **5**, 954–975.

Kingdon J (1997). *Intelligent Systems and Financial Forecasting*, Springer.

Kohonen T (1982). Self-organised formation of topologically correct feature maps, *Biol. Cybern.*, **43**, 59–69.

Kohonen T (1990). The self-organizing map. *Proc. IEEE*, **78**, 1464–1480.

Kramer MA (1991). Nonlinear principal component analysis using autoassociative neural networks. *AIChe Journal*, **37**, 233–243.

LeCun Y, Jackel LD, Graf HP, Boser B, Denker JS, Guyon I, Henderson D, Howard RE, Hubbard W and Solla SA (1990). Optical character recognition and neural-net chips. *Proc. Int. Neural Network Conf, INNC-90*, Paris, 651–655.

Lippmann RP (1987). An introduction to computing with neural nets. *IEEE ASSP Magazine*, April issue, 4–12.

Little RJA and Rubin DB (1987). *Statistical Analysis with Missing Data*. Wiley, New York.

Lowe D (1995). On the use of nonlocal and nonpositive definite basis functions in radial basis function networks. *Proc. 4th IEE Int. Conf. on Artificial Neural Networks*, Cambridge, 206–211.

Lowe D and McLachlan D (1995). Modelling of nonstationary processes using radial basis function networks. *Proc. 4th IEE Int. Conf. on Artificial Neural Networks*, Cambridge, 300–305.

Lowe D and Zapart K (1997). Validation of neural networks in automotive engine calibration. *Proc. 5th IEE Int. Conf. on Artificial Neural Networks*, Cambridge, 221–226.

McCulloch N, Bedworth M and Bridle J (1987). NETspeak: A multi-layer perceptron that can read aloud. *Technical Report RIPRREP 1000/4/87*, RSRE Malvern.

Makhoul J (1975). Linear prediction: a tutorial review. *Proc. IEEE*, **63**, 561–580.

Masters T (1995). *Neural, novel and hybrid algorithms for time series prediction*. Wiley, New York.

Møller M (1993). A scaled conjugate gradient algorithm for fast supervised learning. *Neural Networks*, **6**, 525–533.

Morgan G and Austin J (1995). Safety critical neural networks. *Proc. 4th IEE Int. Conf. on Artificial Neural Networks*, Cambridge, 212–217.

Moody J and Darken CJ (1989). Fast learning in networks of locally-tuned processing units. *Neural Computation*, **1**, 281–294.

Murray AF and Tarassenko L (1994). *Analogue Neural VLSI: A Pulse Stream Approach*. Chapman & Hall, London.

Nairac A, Corbett-Clark T, Ripley R, Townsend N and Tarassenko L (1997a). Choosing an appropriate model for novelty detection. *Proc. 5th IEE Int. Conf. on Artificial Neural Networks*, Cambridge, 117–122.

Nairac A, Townsend N, Carr R, King S, Cowley P and Tarassenko L (1997b). A system for the analysis of jet engine vibration data. *Journal of Computer Aided Engineering*, in press.

Pardey J, Roberts S and Tarassenko L (1996a). A review of parametric modelling techniques for EEG analysis. *Med. Eng. Phys.*, **18**, 2–11.

Pardey J, Roberts S, Tarassenko L. and Stradling J (1996b). A new approach to the analysis of the human sleep/wakefulness continuum. *J. Sleep Res.*, **5**(4), 201–210.

Park J and Sandberg IW (1991). Approximation and radial basis function networks. *Neural Computation*, **3**, 246–257.

Platt J (1991). A resource-allocating network for function interpolation. *Neural Computation*, **3**, 213–225.

Press WH, Teukolsky SA, Vetterling WT and Flannery BP (1992). *Numerical Recipes in C: The Art of Scientific Computing.* 2nd edition. Cambridge University Press, Cambridge.

Rabiner LR and Gold B (1975). *Theory and Application of Digital Signal Processing.* Prentice-Hall, New Jersey.

Ramacher U, Raab W, Anlauf J, Hachmann U, Beichter J, Brüls N, Weßeling M, Sicheneder S, Männer R, Gläß J and Wurz A (1993). Multiprocessor and memory architecture of the neurocomputer SYNAPSE-1. *Proc 3rd Int. Conf. on Microelectronics for Neural Networks*, Edinburgh, 163–174.

Refenes P (1995). *Neural Networks in the Capital Markets*, Wiley, New York.

Richard MD and Lippmann RP (1991). Neural network classifiers estimate Bayesian a-posteriori probabilities. *Neural Computation*, **3**, 461–483.

Ripley BD (1996). *Pattern Recognition and Neural Networks.* Cambridge University Press, Cambridge.

Ripley R, Tarassenko L and Harris AL (1997). Neural network models for breast cancer prognosis. *Neural Computing and Applications*, in press.

Roberts SJ, Tarassenko L (1994). A probabilistic resource allocating network for novelty detection. *Neural Computation*, **6**, 270–284.

Roberts SJ and Tarassenko L (1995). Automated Sleep EEG Analysis using an RBF Network. In: *Applications of Neural Networks*, Murray AF, ed., Kluwer Academic Publishers, 305–322.

Rumelhart DE, Hinton GE and Williams RJ (1986). Learning representations by back-propagating errors. *Nature*, **323**, 533–536.

Sammon JW (1969). A nonlinear mapping for data structure analysis. *IEEE Transactions on Computers*, **18**, 401–409.

Sejnowski TJ and Rosenberg CR (1987). Parallel networks that learn to pronounce English text. *Complex Systems*, **1**, 145–168.

Setiono R (1997). Extracting rules from neural networks by pruning and hidden-unit splitting. *Neural Computation* **9**, 205–225.

Sharpe PK and Solly RJ (1995). Dealing with missing values in neural network-based diagnostic systems. *Neural Computing and Applications*, **3**, 73–77.

Tarassenko L, Tombs JN, Reynolds JH (1991). Neural network architectures for content-addressable memory. *IEE Proceedings Pt F*, **138**, 33–39.

Tarassenko L and Roberts SJ (1994). Supervised and unsupervised learning in radial basis function classifiers. *IEE Proceedings, Vision, Image & Signal Processing*, **141**, 210–216.

Tarassenko L, Hayton P, Cerneaz N and Brady M (1995). Novelty detection for the identification of masses in mammograms. *Proc. 4th IEE Int. Conf. on Artificial Neural Networks*, Cambridge, 442–447.

Tarassenko L, Whitehouse R, Gasparini G and Harris AL (1996). Neural network prediction of relapse in breast cancer patients. *Neural Computing and Applications*, **4**(2), 106–114.

Tibshirani, R (1996). A comparison of some error estimates for neural network models. *Neural Computation*, **8**, 152–163.

Tipping ME and Lowe D (1997). Shadow targets: a novel algorithm for topographic projections by radial basis functions. *Proc. 5th IEE Int. Conf. on Artificial Neural Networks*, Cambridge, 7–12.

Tombs JN (1989). A more representative coding for NETspeak. *Technical Report RIPRREP 1000/69/89*, RSRE Malvern.

Townsend NW and Tarassenko L (1997). Estimations of error bounds for RBF networks. *Proc. 5th IEE Int. Conf. on Artificial Neural Networks*, Cambridge, 227–232.

Weigend AS and Gershenfeld NA (1993). *Time Series Prediction: Forecasting the Future and Understanding the Past*. SFI Studies in the Sciences of Complexity, Proc. Vol. XV, Addison-Wesley.

Werbos PJ (1974). Beyond regression: new tools for prediction and analysis in the behavioural sciences. Ph.D. thesis, Harvard University, Boston, Massachusetts.

Widrow B and Lehr MA (1990). 30 years of adaptive neural networks: perceptron, madaline, and backpropagation. *Proc. IEEE*, **78**, 1415–1442.

Williams CW, Qazaz C, Bishop CM and Zhu H (1995). On the relationship between Bayesian error bars and the input data density. *Proc. 4th IEE Int. Conf. on Artificial Neural Networks*, Cambridge, 160–165.

Index